RAVE OFF

Popular Cultural Studies

Series editors: Justin O'Connor, Steve Redhead and Derek Wynne.

The Manchester Institute for Popular Culture was set up in order to promote theoretical and empirical research in the area of contemporary popular culture, both within the University and in conjunction with local, national and international agencies. The Institute is currently engaged in two major comparative research projects around aspects of consumption and popular culture in the City. The Institute also runs a number of postgraduate research programmes, with a particular emphasis on ethnographic work. The series intends to reflect all aspects of the Institute's activities. Current theoretical debates within the field of popular culture will be explored within an empirical context. Much of the research is undertaken by young researchers actively involved in their chosen fields of study, allowing an awareness of the issues and an attentiveness to actual developments often lacking in standard academic writings on the subject. The series will also reflect the working methods of the Institute, emphasising a collective research effort and the regular presentation of work-in progress to the Institute's research seminars. The series hopes, therefore, both to push forward the debates around popular culture, urban regeneration and postmodern social theory whilst introducing an ethnographic and contextual basis for such debates.

Book titles in the series:

Rave Off: Politics and Deviance in Contemporary Youth Culture
The Passion and the Fashion: Football Fandom in the New Europe

Rave Off

Politics and deviance in contemporary youth culture

edited by
Steve Redhead

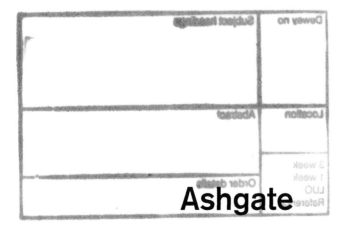
Ashgate

Published by
Ashgate Publishing Limited
Gower House
Croft Road
Aldershot, Hants
GU11 3HR
England

Ashgate Publishing Company
131 Main Street
Burlington, VT 05401-5600 USA

Ashgate website:http://www.ashgate.com

A CIP catalogue record for this book is available from the British Library

ISBN 1 85628 463 8 (Hardback)

Reprinted 1999, 2002

Dewey no	Subject headings
305. 235	Youth culture

Location	Abstract
AID LRC	Drug culture & popular music
3 week 1 week LUO Reference	Order details 693 A7 £40 50

Printed in Great Britain by Biddles Limited, Guildford and King's Lynn

Contents

Preface

This series of papers was produced by a postgraduate research seminar in the Unit for Law and Popular Culture at Manchester Polytechnic, now the Manchester Metropolitan University. The seminar was open to graduate and undergraduate students interested in the topic 'Popular Music, Youth Culture and Cultural Politics'. These accessible and informative essays are significant for their contribution to interdisciplinary interventions in the field of youth culture and popular music. Perspectives from disciplines as diverse as sociology of law, deviance, design, literary criticism, postmodern theory, ethnography and semiotics were employed in the seminar to make sense of the changes in the 1980s and early 1990s which led - once again - to enormous global media hype about British youth culture.

The repository of this renewed media interest in the hedonistic culture of youth in the late twentieth century was, for a time, the city of Manchester (or 'Madchester' as its best known band, the Happy Mondays, christened it). The contradictory images of this media phenomenon - advertised on the cover of *Newsweek* and televised throughout the world - were examined and explained. Moreover, the legal and social regulation of youth culture associated with it, such as the police clampdown on clubs like the Hacienda and Konspiracy, and the statutory outlawing of illegal parties or 'raves' (dubbed 'Acid House' parties by the press long after the 'death' of Acid House), were set in their national and international context.

In addition to regular participants in the seminar, visiting speakers were also invited. The following speakers gave a public seminar as guest lecturers. Our thanks to all those who took part, especially:

Sarah Champion for her talk, Don't Believe the Hype;
Dave Haslam for his talk, There's No Business Like The Music Business; and
Simon Reynolds for his talk, The Politics of Popular Music.

Note: These chapters are a collection of essays. Where possible a house style has been employed (for referencing and so on) but occasionally, where extensive literature search has been carried out, exceptions have been made.

About the authors

Steve Redhead, is author of *The End-of-the-Century Party: Youth and Pop Towards 2000* (Manchester University Press, 1990) and *Football With Attitude:*(Wordsmith, 1991). His first book *Sing When You're Winning:The Last Football Book* (Pluto Press, London, 1987) is now out of print. He is currently preparing a book on the regulation of popular culture entitled *UnpopularCultures* for publication by Manchester University Press. He is Reader in Law and Popular Culture at Manchester Metropolitan University and Director of the Unit for Law and Popular Culture and Joint Director of the Manchester Institute For Popular Culture.

Antonio Melechi, has written a number of articles and essays on youth and club culture, some of which have been published in the journals *New Statesman and Society* and *Marxism Today* . He is currently co-authoring a book on Europe and the Gulf War, and researching a book on Italian Culture and Politics in Post-War Britain. During 1990-2 he was a Research Assistant in the Unit for Law and Popular Culture, Manchester Polytechnic, where he also gained his undergraduate degree in English Studies in 1989.

Hillegonda Rietveld graduated from Manchester Polytechnic in 1991. She is currently the Research Assistant in the Manchester Institute For Popular Culture at Manchester Metropolitan University. As part of her work on contemporary dance culture she has interviewed participants in the Netherlands, England and the United States. She has been an active musician in the area of electronic dance music and was a key member of the seminal early/mid-80s band, Quando Quango. She is the author of the much-cited essay on rave culture, *Living the Dream,* updated in this book, and, in co-operation with writer Jon Savage, has compiled *The Haçienda Must Be Built!* an illustrated book on ten years of the famous Manchester nightclub. She has also written an essay for Sublime, the publication of the Manchester Music and Design Exhibition at Cornerhouse. She is responsible for the co-ordination of an exhibition on dance club culture, *Down At The Club,* which was held at Manchester Polytechnic in September as part of the *In The City* music seminar, and is being shown again in February/March 1993.

Kristian Russell attended the Unit for Law and Popular Culture seminar in 1990-91, and completed the History of Art and Design and Visual Studies course at Staffordshire Polytechnic in 1988-91. Kristian Russell was born in Stockholm, Sweden in 1968 and spent the majority of the 1970s in Stockholm on a diet of Steely Dan, Kiss, Black Uhuru and corduroy flares. He returned to England in 1981 and was schooled at Windsor Boys School (Berkshire) until 1986. A Foundation Course in Art and Design at Brighton Polytechnic followed a year after in 1987. His interest in art and music dates back to his childhood but this has been considerably fuelled by 'finding' psychedelic 60s music in 1988, the 'Second Summer of Love', DJ-ing regularly for two years and a memorable collaboration as a guitarist with an ambient techno act in Staffordshire. He is currently residing in Stockholm illustrating in magazines, being involved with the merchandise industry and freaking out Glam rockers with dub techno at clubs. An ambient funk musical project is currently being prepared.

Patrick Mignon is author of a number of essays and conference papers on football, youth, popular music and drugs. He works at the Institut du Recherche et d'Information Socio-Économique at the Université Paris Dauphine in France. This is the first time his extensive research work has been translated from French into English. He is a member of the advisory board of the Manchester Institute for Popular Culture.

Justin O'Connor is the translator of Patrick Mignon's Chapter in this book. He is Senior Research Fellow at the Manchester Institute for Popular Culture. He is one of the academic series editors of *Popular Cultural Studies*.

1 The end of the end-of-the-century party

Steve Redhead

Youth cultures appear to have succeeded each other in Britain over a fifty year period since the mid-40s. There are archaeologies - or histories - in existence of previous youth subcultures before this era but something marks out the distinctive post-war youth styles. In this period a specifically youth 'style' became commodified as consumer culture progressively swamped the advanced economies of the West (and latterly the more 'backward' East): British youth cultural styles were exported around the globe as once the country's manufactured goods had been. By the 80s 'Youth Culture' had become an industry in itself and it was even argued by some that youth was no longer about rebellion or revolt but constituted merely a marketing device and advertisers' fiction. For others this had always been the case. One writer, Toby Young, later to become one of the editors of the 90s populist journal of popular culture *The Modern Review*, proclaimed in 1985 in the now defunct magazine *New Society* that "the term youth culture is at best of historical value only since the customs and mores associated with it have been abandoned by your actual young person." Whether or not this is true, youth cultural tourism is still rife; in the UK, it is seen as part of the nation's heritage and ever more cities vie for tourists on the basis of their respective pop music and youth culture histories - for instance, Merseyside and The Beatles, Manchester and Happy Mondays and so on.

The End-of-the-Century Party, published in 1990 by Manchester University Press, was a provisional theoretical account of youth and pop at the *fin-de-siecle*. It radically reworked what had become the orthodox approaches to global pop culture by the end of the 80s. It questioned a particular 'linear' way of thinking about the connections between pop and youth culture which was becoming ever more difficult to sustain, and suggested fresh lines of enquiry. *Rave Off* follows on from such tentative questioning of the application of contemporary cultural theory (especially around the concepts of postmodernity and postmodernism) to the historical development of youth culture. It seeks to expose some of the problems involved in 'postmodern' theorising of 'postmodernity'. Focusing on 'rave' culture in the late 80s and early 90s, the essays collected here are all grounded in ethnographic participant observation research which recall earlier forays into youth culture and youth subcultures by the Centre for Contemporary Cultural Studies (CCCS) at the University of Birmingham in the 1970s, which in turn grew out of the research into politics and deviance by the National Deviancy Conference (NDC) in the late 60s and early 70s. Inevitably, these current essays radically question that 70s Cultural Studies legacy whilst owing an enormous debt to the pioneering work of those earlier ethnographic studies.

The story in that legacy (plundered by all manner of cultural critics ever since) told, essentially, of an evolutionary unfolding of post-war youth cultures. Beginning, initially, with the teddy boy style (culled largely from the late 40s Edwardian look) in the early/mid-50s, working class subcultures have been retrospectively mapped back onto British cultural history every few years by fashion and music journalists and entrepreneurs eager to perpetuate some enduring myths about some spectacular subcultures. The mods, seen to spring from a more semi-skilled and white collar social base than the teds, came on to the youth cultural landscape to clash, metaphorically and literally, with unskilled rockers especially at holiday beaches (Clacton, Brighton, Hastings) in the mid-60s. Greasers, bikers and other variants of bike boys in leather jackets (epitomised first by Marlon Brando in the 50s film The Wild One) emerged eventually, though with nothing like the legendary menace of the American breed, the Hells Angels. Mod itself, on the other hand, prefigured many varieties of British youth culture for the foreseeable future. Skinheads, metamorphosed 'hard' mods, were spotted fighting other teams' 'crews' at football matches in the season after England's World Cup soccer victory in 1966, before they too splintered eventually, in the early 70s, into crombies, suedeheads and other groupings, but not before skins had become infamous for their attacks on gays and blacks, as well as a perverse penchant for ska music, the precursor of reggae. Glamrock united these remnants with a hippie style which itself had been created from 'soft' mod styles in 1967. Perhaps most controversially of all punks in 1976-7 were held to be the natural inheritors of a dole-queue ethos (unemployment rose to over a million in the mid-70s). Punk style was much more likely to have originated in the arts schools rather than the 'street', however. The casuals, emphasising 'smart', expensive clothes from sports or mens wear, took their place in this youth culture museum from a complex of mod, soulboy and a look modelled on the influential singer, David Bowie, around the time punk was promoting 'ripped and torn', Nazi insignia and bondage gear. Casual style was mainstream and ubiquitous in Britain by the late 1980s but such one-dimensional freeze-framing hid a complex and ever changing street style which has rarely been documented outside fanzines or, much later, by style magazines like *Blitz, The Face, Arena* or *i-D*.

More middle class styles such as the beats in the 50s as well as the hippies in the late 60s were fitted in on the same historical plane. These youth subcultural fashions were usually read as white styles; some urban black styles - rudies, Rastas, B-Boys and ragga(muffin)s - did however receive a similar kind of treatment in pop histories on a parallel time scale. In truth British youth styles *always* owed a debt to either developments in black styles or black music - CCCS' Dick Hebdige in his classic Cultural Studies book *Subculture* even described punk as "white ethnicity" - as they did to changes in gay culture. The absence of women in these youth culture narratives began to be repaired from the mid-70s both in terms of previous subcultural histories - which histories could be revised to include their previously hidden presence - and a more observant notation of their role in post-punk subcultures. Subsequent revivals of these 'original' youth styles failed to disturb the orthodoxy that this was an unfolding progression of youth style upon youth style. Only in the 80s did this linear process receive a critical look. Music led styles such as heavy metal boys (and girls), goths, new romantics, acid housers or ravers dominated the 80s as cultural critics constantly sought the 'new punk'. Acid House or rave culture was misread in this fashion, when in reality it looked to roots in the club-based Northern soul (all dayers, all nighters) of the 70s and was in fact notorious for mixing all kinds of styles on the same dance floor and attracting a range of previously opposed subcultures from football hooligans to New Age hippies, a phenomenon caught in Steve Redhead's illustrated account *Football with Attitude* published in Manchester by Wordsmith in 1991.

As the end-of-the-century approaches a 'hedonism in hard times' is perhaps the best way to describe a sea of youth styles circulating and re-circulating in a harsh economic and political climate where youth is increasingly seen once again (after Margaret Thatcher in Britain at least) as a source of fear for employed, respectable society and a 'law and order' problem for the police. New youth cultures such as ravers and crusties (a label for a motley collection of travellers, New Age Hippies, anarcho-punks with dogs on strings) have revived the debates about 'folk devils' and 'moral panics' which Stan Cohen had first identified in the 60s in his *Folk Devils and Moral Panics*, a study of the creation of the mods and rockers. As *The End-of-the-Century Party* explains at some length, neither 60s deviancy theory or 70s versions of Cultural Studies can satisfactorily account for global changes in youth and youth subcultures since the punk era. Moreover, these theoretical explanations - despite many original insights and their basis in much stimulating ethnographic research - look ever more fragile in their claims to explain youth culture *at the time:* that is in the pre-punk era of the 50s, 60s and early 70s. One tendency amongst sociologists of youth and deviance has been to respond with a revived liberal sociological positivist theory which was popular in America and (to some extent) Britain in the 50s and mid-60s before the turn to radicalism of the new left, and subsequently, the new right took its hold. Terence Morris, a leading exponent of such thinking in criminology in Britain since the 50s, recently offered(1) the view that the emergence of folk devils of the 90s such as ravers/New Age Travellers could be put down to a sociological determinism: that is, unemployment and other structural economic conditions of recent liberal capitalism *necessarily* had caused the growth of a youthful underclass - that in no way *chose* its fate - which in turn posed a threat to the British Prime Minister John Major's vision of a contented classless society. Changes in social policy were required in Morris' view to repair these sorts of structural dysfunctions.

The End-of-the-Century Party title was originally sampled fromJean Baudrillard - capturing both the moods of celebration and nostalgia which the *'fin-de-siecle'* had seemingly generated - who

4

over the last decade has been rediscovered as some kind of 'postmodernist', a philosopher par excellence of the 'post'. 'Postmodernism' in all its myriad (dis)guises has been the terrain for many theorists of deviance dissatisfied with all of the above approaches to youth culture in the 80s and 90s. Baudrillard himself has always rejected such a label, and two(2) recent studies make a very good case for his reasoned resistance to 'postmodern theory'. Nevertheless, as the studies in the following Chapters establish, without in any way *applying* some grand narrative derived from Baudrillard, contemporary media-saturated ('postmodern') youth culture can be excavated by way of some of Baudrillard's signposts. Baudrillard may not have been much given to the culture of the nightclub but that does not mean that lively ethnography cannot meet contemporary cultural theory without a lasting analytical benefit.

The studies in this book are all analyses of the development of what, since 1987, has been described as 'Acid House' or 'rave' culture. These changes in youth culture are by no means representative of the whole of contemporary youth culture but they are at the cutting edge of 'politics and deviance'. The Chapters range over questions such as: are recreational drugs such as Ecstacy a passing fad or part of a wider transformation in youth and popular culture? what is/was Acid House or rave culture? how does it differ from previous youth cultures in the 50s, 60s, 70s and 80s? is it in conformity with mainstream values in politics and society (such as materialism, enterprise, success, tourism) or deviant from them? what had the phenomenon which the global media labelled 'Madchester' got to do with it? where does youth culture go from here?

Sources

1.   Interviewed in July 1992 on BBC Radio 4 *Today* programme and developed in subsequent newspaper contributions.

2.   Gane, M. (1991), *Baudrillard: Critical and Fatal Theory*, and *Baudrillard's Bestiary*, published in paperback by Routledge, London.There has always been a relationship between club culture and drugs...only now there are a hell of a lot more clubbers and they take a hell of a lot more drugs. (Stuart Cosgrove, quoted by Sean O'Hagan in *The Times Saturday Review*, February 22, 1992).

2 The politics of Ecstacy

Steve Redhead

Hence we move to the form of ecstasy. Ecstasy is that quality
specific to each body that spirals in on itself until it has lost all
meaning, and thus radiates on pure and empty form. Fashion
is the ecstasy of the beautiful: the pure and empty form of a
spiralling aesthetics. Simulation is the ecstasy of the real. To
prove this, all you need do is watch television, where real
events follow one another in a perfectly ecstatic relation, that
is to say through vertiginous and stereotyped traits, unreal and
recurrent, which allow the continuous and uninterrupted
juxtapositions. Ecstatic: such is the object of advertising, and
such is the consumer in the eyes of advertising." Jean
Baudrillard, quoted in Mark Poster (ed): *Jean Baudrillard:
Selected Writings* (Polity, Oxford, 1988, p. 187).

Discourse on drugs, and, particularly, discourse about Ecstacy or
MDMA or 'E' has, to date, generally been about drugs as
'pathology'. In this Chapter I want to concentrate on discourses
about a drug which is seen (in Britain) by its users (who are often also
its dealers) as 'recreational'. It can be used and usually not affect the
person's ability to work the next, or the following, day. It is
associated with a politics of pleasure, a hedonism (in hard times) - a
pleasure for its own sake in times when moral regulation of youth is
pervasive and deep economic recession is rife. It takes its place on a
continuum *not* of drugs/alcohol but of legal/illegal substances. It is
discourses on drugs which produce drugs as a problem not the other
way around. Drugs as a problem, as an object of study are not a
given in the way that positivists would have us believe. (1) Finally, as

an introductory remark, I want to stress *legal* discourse. In my view, law polices both the boundaries of its own discourse *and* the boundaries of other discourses (e.g. popular and youth culture, postmodernism, etc.). What law regulates and disciplines is the contours of the 'social', a realm which, for Jean Baudrillard, has tended to disappear in recent history.

The 80s in Britain began with moral panics about hard drug use (for instance, heroin, and later 'crack' cocaine) amongst youth in working class estates of large cities. The mid-80s saw panics about hard drug use (especially around issues of prostitution and the sharing of needles) and its role in the spread of AIDS. The late 80s and early 90s have witnessed panics about 'lager louts' as well as old psychedelic drugs such as LSD, soft drugs such as cannabis and new, 'designer' drugs such as Ecstacy or 'E' (MDMA). This chapter examines some of the discourses and practices of 'government' - as Michel Foucault has termed it - which sustained just one of these diverse panics. It draws on local archival and ethnographic research into legal and social regulation of contemporary British youth culture.(2)

Ecstasy

Ecstacy or Ecstasy, often called 'E', 'ADAM' or 'XTC' is known chemically as 3, 4 Methylenedioxymethamphetamine, or MDMA for short. The oils from such diverse plants as nutmeg, dill, parsley seed, calamus, crocus, saffron, vanilla beans and sassafras all contain the chemical precursors of MDMA. However, more often than not, MDMA is produced synthetically in a laboratory from Methamphetamine. According to the *Mersey Drugs Journal*, Vol. 2 No. 4, "a potted history of the drug looks like this":

1914: Scientists develop MDMA while searching for an appetite suppressant for soldiers during the First World War. It is patented by Merck Pharmaceutical Company and then virtually forgotten about for forty years.

1953: The US Army Medical Centre experiment on mammals with MDMA.

1962: Alexander Shuglin extracts myristicin from the oils of nutmeg and mace, then synthesises myristicin into MDMA.

1976: The first report on the psychoactive effects of MDMA appear in the scientific literature.

1977: Reports of MDMA being sold on the black market in the USA. Made illegal in UK (Misuse of Drugs Act 1971).

1980: MDMA starts to become popular amongst drug users in the USA.

1985: MDMA is made a Schedule 1 controlled substance in the USA, despite opposition from Psychiatrists who have been using it as a therapeutic tool.

1988: MDMA becomes popular in London and other major English cities, along with the 'Acid House' club scene selling at £15 to £30 a tablet.

Ecstasy in Britain

In October 1985, an article in *The Face* magazine declared that MDMA had been coming into Britain in small quantities since the beginning of the decade. Since 1985 seizures of the drug by the police have steadily increased and, in early 1987, came the first evidence that MDMA was being manufactured in Britain after a raid on an illicit laboratory in West London. To most people MDMA has been associated with night clubs in various parts of the country that play 'Acid House', 'rave' or 'dance culture' music which was prevalent from around 1985, but especially since 1988.

The summer of 1987 saw the first widespread use of Ecstasy in the major cities of Britain. That date also earmarked Ecstasy's 10th year as an illegal Class A substance (with the same potential penalties as heroin and cocaine) in Britain.

Although many people would argue that the passion and the fashion for 'Acid House' no longer exists, dance music and club life still plays an increasingly prominent part in the life styles and tastes of many of today's youth in Britain. Similarly, MDMA, far from being an 'expensive and short lived fad', has quickly established itself as a major part of certain drug using circles in Britain.

Our research into Ecstasy use has suggested the following differences between opiate and non-opiate drug use, though it should be noted that some of our focus has been on users who have seen fit to approach drugs agencies, having defined their 'E' use as a problem. In general, as well as the setting there are many difference between Ecstasy use in Britain and the use of drugs such as heroin or cocaine. As of early 1991 it could be said that:

a)   Ecstasy is an outdoor drug.

b)   Ecstasy is easily digested, it does not involve complex rituals of preparation and ingestion.

c)   Ecstasy is used recreationally (there is little evidence to show that the drug may be addictive).

d)   Ecstasy users tend to disassociate themselves from opiate drug users (whom they themselves see as 'junkies').

e)   Ecstasy is a weekend drug; there is little evidence to show that ravers are using Ecstasy (or for that matter any drugs) during the week, or more specifically when not engaged in leisure pursuits.

f)   Ecstasy use is now widespread amongst many social groups (for instance some sections of youth who regularly attend football matches).

g)   The legal problems encountered by Ecstasy users are vastly different from other drug users.

h)   Ecstasy has not produced many of the attendant symptoms associated with other drugs. In the context of 14 deaths from 'E' in Britain, the consensus of anecdotal evidence is that MDMA is generally safe; that is, users rarely seem to suffer any untoward consequences. This means that the traditional indicators of illicit drug use - such as emergency room admissions, overdose deaths, treatment, programme admissions and arrests - will not reflect much in the way of MDMA's actual usage.

i)   The greatest problem facing consumers of Ecstasy is quality control. In an industry not particularly well known for its benevolence, relationships between a vast amount of predominantly culturally 'unsophisticated' consumers and producers (i.e. dealers) are continually open to all manner of exploitation and mistrust.

'E' is for ever?

No one is quite sure just how many people are using Ecstasy regularly in this country, though some put the number who have tried 'E' at 1 million. This should come as no surprise for there is little worthwhile information regarding Ecstasy available despite a plethora of recent studies of the drug MDMA, especially in the USA.

Estimates on usage vary widely.   However, researchers now believe that a "significant" number of young people in England are familiar with what has been generically termed 'dance drugs'. Russell Newcombe argues that,

> Every weekend in the North West of England, an estimated 20 to 30 thousand people go to House Music clubs and parties, known as 'raves'. Several thousand take drugs such as cannabis, ecstasy, amphetamine, and/or LSD.[3]

Similarly, research carried out in Brighton "showed that 62% of those who regularly go to night-clubs said they had used drugs recently".[4]   The Brighton study concludes that "use of drugs is considered by many young Pleasuredomers as a valid component of their leisure, along with their dress, style, choice of friends, music and clubs." Other drug researchers argue that "Ecstasy (MDMA, 3, 4 Methylenedioxymethamphetamine - or to the ravers, just 'E') is the ravers' cultural choice."[5]

Ecstasy has also made its presence felt in many different ways, for instance it has become almost synonymous with what has become know as 'Madchester', which some people would argue has been the most creative and influential force in British youth culture since the 'Punk Explosion' of the mid/late 70s. It has also dominated contemporary pop music; references to 'E' permeate much of today's music: for example New Order's reference to "E is for England" in *World in Motion* and ED 209's *Acid to Ecstasy*. Ecstasy is also proving important for some young people. 'E' is increasingly replacing more traditional drugs such as Marijuana and LSD in becoming their introduction to illegal drug use. Not surprisingly, therefore, there have been many fears expressed about 'E', fears concerning its chemical make up, its after-effects, both short and long term, and its *alleged* involvement in the escalation of crime related activity amongst certain so-called 'drug gangs' on the streets of Manchester and other cities.

However, it is 'E's relationship with 'Acid House' and 'Acid House' parties that has produced most alarm about the drug, especially amongst the media. Following on from Stan Cohen's seminal work in the 60s and 70s on the mods and rockers phenomena, (6) it has been argued that 'E' and 'Acid' have produced a moral panic in society. Users have been attributed many of the characteristics of previous folk devils. As this panic swept Britain during the late 80s it assumed tragic proportions when a "pretty" 16 year old girl died outside a famous Manchester night club (The Haçienda) after allegedly taking 'E'. The ensuing media uproar (in this case both local and national) and the consequent legal battle to shut the aforementioned club condemned for the foreseeable future the character of both 'E' and 'Acid'. However, not everyone joined in this holy crusade against the newest of youth culture evils: MDMA has always had its defenders including many doctors, scientists and academics (not least of whom was R. D. Laing) who were ready to enter the debate over the characterisation of 'E'. There has also been the often neglected voice of 'E' users themselves, for the latter half of the 80s has witnessed a plethora of literature produced by club goers themselves for other club goers. For many of these people the pleasures of 'E' far and away outstripped any potential dangers that the drug may possess; thus amongst many club goers 'E' became known as the friendly drug, though by 1990 many of 'E' 's most vociferous supporters were "lamenting the idea of a drug infested weekend...come Monday morning", as *Boys Own* fanzine put it. Nevertheless, drug use amongst young people in Britain, especially Ecstasy, is now so widespread that it can no longer be adequately explained by either subcultural theory or traditional notions of deviance.

In particular, to de-contextualize Ecstasy use in Britain from its predominant setting within what has loosely been called rave culture is both unrewarding and misleading. It is clear that Ecstasy and rave culture go hand in glove; there may well be an internal argument amongst aficionados over which came first, but to most ravers they are inseparable. Consider the following quotes:

'E' is the key to the music.

Ecstasy changed the country like acid in the 60s. When you take it, it changes your whole life.

House is not just the music, its a state of mind.

People no longer wanted to sit and pontificate. They wanted to move and be moved. Shag, shag, shag. Dance, dance, dance.

A Mancunian generation hell bent on hedonism and hooked on a lifestyle as self-assured and self-possessed as it is anti-liberal...White working class terrace sub-culture indulging in casual drug-taking on a scale not seen since their parents did it 20 years before.... (7)

As always the British media were alert to the relationship between the twin evils of 'Acid House parties' and Ecstasy. The mass media had a veritable field day with some of the key features of what it perceived to be a new youth style or subculture, to rival punk in the 1970s or hippy in the 1960s. An enticing shopping list was laid out for the intending acid houser or raver including 1960s psychedelia, Ecstasy and other hallucinogenic drugs such as LSD, Smiley logos, fluorescent paraphernalia, pastel colours and Lucozade. The newspaper headlines, which persisted for years since the Second Summer of Love, "summer of 88", tell their own story of the law and order reaction which has taken place:

ACID CRACKDOWN
ACID HOUSE THREAT RAPPED
LUSH LIFE LURE THAT SNARED ECSTASY GIRL
(over a report on an Ecstasy drugs smuggling court case)
'WE'LL CRACK ACID OUTLAWS' - POLICE
ACID HOUSE POLICE IN TERROR CHASE

HELICOPTER SWOOPS ON MOTORWAY ACID
HOUSE PARTY
POLICE ROUT PARTY RIOTERS

The Haçienda story - A precautionary tale

The specific media narrative of moral panic I want to relate here concerns a case study of the Haçienda nightclub in Manchester. Since its opening in 1982, the club, part owned by the band New Order and Factory Communications boss and television personality Anthony H. Wilson, transformed a former yachting warehouse into a major youth cultural tourist attraction for the city and an icon of European clubland. Tim Booth, lead singer of James, told the *New Musical Express* on August 4, 1990, that the "Haçienda is Manchester's Eiffel Tower". Even notorious British tabloid newspapers like *The Sun* have rightly described the club as, at some time in the late 80s, the most important Northern English venue since the Cavern in Liverpool in the era of Beatlemania; furthermore, in January 1991 the club was the winner of the Best Venue in Britain award. Internationally famous pop groups such as the Stone Roses, and especially Factory Records' hottest property the Happy Mondays, became associated with the club by playing and being seen there; current global megastar Madonna played an early gig there in 1984. However, apart from the history of the Haçienda as a physical space it is also a cultural space with a history; it is the latter that I am concerned with in this chapter. In particular, the Haçienda has acted as an intersection for a variety of "discursive formations" - in Michel Foucault's phrase - which in my view produce the 'objects' for analysis, such as illegal drug use and contemporary youth deviance in general.

Part of the international media notoriety associated with the Haçienda is the event in July 1989 - already referred to - which resulted in the death of a sixteen year old girl, Claire Leighton. Ms Leighton had collapsed after reportedly taking a tablet of Ecstasy bought by a friend in the Haçienda. The inquest into her death heard that she had developed a rare reaction to the drug. In any case, her sad demise constituted the first known fatality (or first "Acid House fatality" as some journalists had it) as a result of Ecstasy use in Britain. In February 1990 a new piece of national legislation came

14

into force in the Greater Manchester area, namely the Licensing Act, 1988. This gave the police greater discretionary powers to object to the granting of licences to nightclubs by local magistrates, who were themselves empowered to revoke licences at any time during their currency. Licensing hearings were to be more frequent so that the Justices of the Peace (magistrates) who sat on the sessions would have more opportunity to revoke licences than they had before the Act came into force. Several of the city's clubs were to close as part of the Operation Clubwatch set up by Greater Manchester Police in early 1990. For instance, in December 1990, Konspiracy (which had taken over from the Haçienda as the punters most favoured venue) lost its licence after "police told magistrates of drugs dealing on the premises, and the management admitted that some of the North West's most dangerous gangsters often mingled with the club's customers" (*Manchester Evening News*, January 31, 1991). In September 1990, after police had already taken a decision to oppose Konspiracy's licence, they locked "600 revellers inside...after a dance floor stabbing" of a student; the *Manchester Evening News* reported that everyone in the club was questioned during a four hour police investigation while surgeons saved the young man's life ("Dancers Quizzed in Night Club Horror", September 18, 1990). On another occasion the *Manchester Evening News* claimed that undercover police had been in the club previously and were offered LSD ('Acid') and counted 62 people smoking cannabis. Another club, Precinct 13, lost its licensing hearing at the magistrates' court in January 1991 "ostensibly because it didn't serve hot food as specified in its licence, though the club had food, cooking equipment and plates. The police said they were refused a hot meal when they dropped in unannounced" (*City Life*, January 17-31, 1991). Significantly, whilst Operation Clubwatch was closing clubs in Greater Manchester, licensing and policing policy in other regions was becoming more liberal. On September 8, 1990, *New Musical Express* reported that in London

> ...both Brixton's Fridge club and Soho's Wag club have been given extended licenses so that they may open until dawn with others set to follow, making the necessity and expense of searching out illegal, and often unsafe, warehouse raves a thing of the past.

Such 'legalisation' of the rave (or as the tabloids persisted in calling it, Acid House) scene was more in line with some of the countries in Continental Europe(8) which British club goers were increasingly visiting, either as tourists, or overnight travelling clubbers when their own British venue (such as Manchester's Haçienda, or later, the nearby Boardwalk, a club based in a building which once housed a Victorian school) took up monthly residency in a city such as Paris. (9)

The Haçienda itself was under covert Greater Manchester Police surveillance from before the time of Claire Leighton's death: an undercover operation monitored, in particular, the use and sale of drugs - mostly cannabis and Ecstasy - in the club for twelve months prior to February 1990 by which time the Licensing Act, passed in 1988, could be eventually applied.

The police soon raised objections to the Haçienda's (and, as we have seen, other clubs') licence, applying to magistrates for the venue's closure "on the grounds that it was frequented by people who blatantly used and dealt with drugs and that the premises were ill-conducted" (*Manchester Evening News*, January 30, 1991). The Haçienda quickly hired one of the top barristers in the country, George Carman, QC, who had gained a popular reputation for defending the likes of comedian Ken Dodd, Liberal politician Jeremy Thorpe and Coronation Street television star Peter Adamson. The licensing hearing before magistrates was twice postponed, while at the second, on July 23, 1990, Carman "pledged that the club would work closely with the police in the meantime to 'declare war' on drug abuse and drug dealing in the Haçienda", revealing that, in what he called an "unprecedented move", both Manchester's Lord Mayor and the Labour leader of the city council, Graham Stringer, had written letters in support of the club's aims and status. Stringer had, in fact, written to say that the Haçienda made a significant contribution to active use of the city centre core". The police solicitor supplied evidence of "70 incidents" uncovered by secret police surveillance in the club; Carman's argument for an adjournment until January 3, 1991, was based on the fact that such a weight of police evidence would take much longer to deal with than the few days set aside in July. The magistrates concurred. The Haçienda immediately printed a 'licence update' flyer for free distribution to punters in the city, which read:

The Haçienda licence hearing on July 23, resulted in the case being adjourned until January 3, 1991. This means that the Haçienda will remain open as usual until this date. FAC 51, The Haçienda, now intends to redouble its efforts to keep our club open. This must involve the complete elimination of controlled drugs on the premises. In this we continue to rely upon your help and co-operation. Please do not, repeat NOT, buy or take drugs in the club, and do not bring drugs onto the premises. Please make sure everyone understands how important this message is. Thank you for your support.

Importantly, by July 1990, the Haçienda as a physical space was far less important to the region's dance culture than it had been, say, in the 'Summer of Love' in 1988; other legal clubs, and more significantly, illegal s at various locations in and around East Lancashire towns like Blackburn and Burnley, and on the motorways towards Stoke-on-Trent had, for some months, been much bigger attractions. By October, 1990, despite a summer tour of American cities by Haçienda DJ's (contributing to a public opinion finding that 40% of New Yorkers made Manchester the UK city they most wanted to visit) audiences had declined and one of its most prominent DJ's, Dave Haslam, announced he was leaving. Nevertheless, 1990 was, for the Haçienda, a year of unparalleled global media exposure. It was, typically, seen by *Newsweek* (where "Madchester: Britain's Feel-Good Music Movement" was the cover feature) in mid-July as the epicentre of the nation's youth culture. Journalist Jennifer Foote describing it as "the city's original music laboratory" in an article which focused on members of a European youth culture still unborn in the "original Summer of Love in 1967" and now "often stoned out of their gourds on the designer drug - Ecstasy". Manchester, and inevitably the Haçienda, was big news and every facet of its iconography was plundered by the world's media, and, where possible, by the city's most entrepreneurial citizens. Culturally, in 1990, the Haçienda had come to represent the unrepresentable, a many-sided free-floating sign with no (real) referent at that moment of historical time.

When it came to the eventual hearing early in January 1991, there was media consternation at the 'six month reprieve' handed out by the city's licensing magistrates. *The Guardian* of January 4, 1991, reported "that the club...is to be allowed to stay open despite police claims that it had been used for drug taking" because magistrates

17

heard "there had been 'a positive change in direction'". The court hearing resulted in a further adjournment of the case, which had been expected to take four weeks, until July 1991 "after solicitors representing the police and the club agreed to put to the test a pledge by the Haçienda to declare war on drug abuse" the *Manchester Evening News* noted on January 3. Evidence that police had made 100 secret visits to the club between February 1989 and July 1990 was quoted by the *Manchester Metro News* as leading to the court allegations that "police had alleged that customers regularly smoked and prepared cannabis reefers and that the smell of cannabis was obvious inside the building." The club's licensee, Paul Mason, was quoted as saying that "the directors (of the Haçienda) are delighted with the opportunity to maintain better standards at the club. The problems we have experienced at the club are part of a wider problem which affects licensed premises in this city".

What seemed to persuade the magistrates that there should be a six month 'trial period' for the Haçienda was the improved relations between the club's management and the Greater Manchester police. Nigel Copeland, solicitor for the Haçienda, said at the January 3 hearing that the Haçienda did not accept the police allegations of drug use at the venue but agreed that there had been "better relationships between the two sides of late". The *New Musical Express* of January 11, 1991, claimed that some "sources in Manchester suggested this week that the police may even drop the case in July if they're satisfied with the club's attitude towards the local drug war". In the event this is exactly what eventually happened - the police did drop the case in summer 1991.

A savage twist in the (false) conclusion to this (pre)cautionary tale was, however, still to occur. Within a month of the 'reprieve' from the city's magistrates, the Haçienda management had announced an abrupt, though temporary closure (the club re-opened to huge attendant publicity in May 1991 and celebrated its tenth birthday in May 1992) of the venue. Anthony H. Wilson declared that "it is with the greatest reluctance that for the moment we are turning the lights out on what is, for us, a most important place". (*Manchester Metro News*, February 1, 1991). The Manchester Evening News headlined the reasons for closure as "Haçienda Closes After Gun Terror". (January 30, 1991). Wilson was quoted as saying "we are sick of the violence and until we can run the club in a safe manner it will be closed". Both papers were clear that "drug-linked" gang rivalry, mainly between gangs from Cheetham Hill and Moss Side (10) were behind the decision; on the re-opening night in May police had to, once again, deter gang members from causing problems for the club. Anthony Wilson confirmed to me, in interview, as early as June 1990, that for several months previously he had been trying to persuade the Greater Manchester Police to move against the impending threat of the drug gang wars in the city. By January 1991, apparently, he could no longer afford to wait for serious injury to befall staff at the club. *The Independent* ("Gun Gangs Force Night Club to Close", January 31, 1991) concluded that the decision followed "an incident on (the previous Saturday evening when a gang threatened the door manager with a handgun" and an incident "on New Year's Eve when a shot was fired in the club when two gangs squared up, though no one was hurt"; the article suggested that "it was violence, rather than drugs, which finally led to the Haçienda's closure". (11) By this time, tabloid newspaper publicity about Manchester gang warfare was at its peak. Papers like the *Daily Express* had, since the summer of 1990, described 'drug gang wars' in the city in language which conflated heroin and cocaine use and sale with cannabis, LSD and Ecstasy use and sale, referring to both ends of the spectrum as "hard drugs". Apart from an interview with former Deputy Chief Constable of Greater Manchester Police, John Stalker, who clearly stated in an interview on television that at that time the drug wars in the city had nothing to do with the drugs being taken in 'trendy clubs' and were confined to conflict over organised heroin and 'crack' cocaine deals, most media accounts made no distinction between 'soft' and 'hard' drugs. Also, 'serious' newspapers such as *The Independent On Sunday* ran stories of 'shock horror' about the 'decline' of Manchester; overnight seemingly 'Madchester' had become 'Badchester'! William Leith, in the most notorious of these features (headed "After Ecstasy" under the byline "What Went Wrong in Manchester: A Drug Economy in Recession") linked crime and music explicitly, referring to "the deranged throb of Acid music" ("Acid House sounds horrible without drugs") and quoting (second hand from i-D magazine) Shaun Ryder, lead singer of the Happy Mondays, as saying the fans "were all on 'E' because we used to go out in the audience selling 'E' like T-shirts".

A partial closure to the 'Haçienda story' which I have excavated, and retold here, was provided by a second local Ecstasy death in May 1991. This, all media accounts made clear, had nothing to do with the

Haçienda. *The Guardian* of May 14, 1991, reported that "Robert Parsonage, aged 18" was "a student who died after an Acid House party" and "had taken the drug Ecstasy" according to police. Mr. Parsonage had, said the *Manchester Evening News* of May 14, 1991, "swallowed five tablets of the drug Ecstasy" at a "legal Acid House party" in Stalybridge, Greater Manchester, and was found at 4 a.m. collapsed outside the sports centre where the event was held; he died from internal bleeding 12 hours later. The *Manchester Evening News* of May 13, 1991, announced on its front page that there had been a "drug tragedy at legal Acid House party": where "Love Pills Kill A Perfect Son". The event's organiser was quoted as saying "It is horrendous for someone to lose their life...but if legal events were stopped because of this it will drive people into the hands of people who organise illegal events without any thoughts of safety".

Rave off

For both legal and illegal parties, the legislative position itself is becoming increasingly complex. Even though the law - in a literal sense - does not 'know' its 'subject', it has had a considerable influence on certain developments in the musical and cultural form of house music. The police and government have reacted in such a way to what was defined (by them) as 'Acid House parties' that a particular form of house music which was associated with the parties was brought into prominence in the public consciousness through such media as press and television (national radio services initially tried to put an unsuccessful ban on 'Acid House').

From 1982 the main law involved was the Public Entertainment Act which required anyone to have a licence if they wished to hold public entertainment. 'Private' parties, particularly from the autumn of 1988 onwards, frequently escaped criminalisation, precisely by being defined as private, as opposed to public, in various court cases. However, an obscure 1967 statute, the Private Places of Entertainments Act, was soon mobilised because it required that any private entertainment done for financial gain must have a licence. Many local authorities had not even adopted this 1967 Act (which they were bound to do if it was to be used in their area) but once the media publicity about Ecstasy/AcidHouse/rave culture reached overdrive the situation started to change. Further, as we have seen, the Licensing Act, 1988, awarded the police greater powers to monitor premises and increased the licensing sessions from once a year to seven. Legislation has been passed to control raves/parties in the previously 'illegal' sector. The Entertainments (Increased Penalties) Acts, 1990, began life as a Private Member's legislative measure given full support by the then Prime Minister Margaret Thatcher's government, thus increasing its chances of parliamentary progress. The Bill, sponsored by back bench Conservative MP for Luton South, Graham Bright (PPS to John Major) successfully completed its passage through the House of Commons, comprising a total of three readings and a committee stage, without opposition. It came into force on July 13, 1990. It increased the penalties for holding an unlicensed public entertainment so that the courts have the power to impose a fine of up to £20,000 for each proven offence or to sentence those responsible to prison for up to six months, or both. The effect of this measure, given the restrictions being imposed on legal clubs, has been to potentially criminalise a whole section of the youth population.

The amphetamine-based 'designer drug' Ecstasy, or MDMA, is, of course, an illegal drug. In Britain, since 1977, it has been one of the 'controlled drugs' classified under the Misuse of Drugs Act, 1971. On May 31, 1987, Ecstasy was made a Schedule 1 controlled substance in the USA, despite opposition from therapists who had been using it in their work.[12] Through its association with a 'new psychedelia' in youth culture in the late 80s and 90s it has inevitably been placed in a position of instrumental centrality ('Ecstasy causes Acid House' in youth culture as some commentators put it, and so on) in much the same way that LSD was viewed as a 'mindbending' catalyst in the counter-culture of the late 1960s. Weight has been given to this argument by the supposed connection between 'Acid' gurus of the 1960s such as Timothy Leary (author of the seminal *The Politics of Ecstasy*) and the new 'Love Labs' of the rave generation, despite Leary's "current playing down past predictions of a drug-led world revolution" and his preference for dabbling in "less high-risk speculations on cryonic speculations and 'virtual reality'".[13]

In my view it is misguided to attribute Ecstasy such a deterministic role in this 'new' politics of hedonistic youth (usually compared unfavourably to the politics of the 1960s psychedelia) of the 80s and 90s.

'E' is for enterprise

The Independent (March 3, 1990) gave space to Tony Colston-Hayter, one of the most prominent entrepreneurs on the dance parties scene, due to his involvement with the companies Sunrise and Back to the Future and his role as Chair of the pressure group, the Association of Dance Party Promoters. Colston-Hayter, who gained nationwide publicity for his business by throwing water over pop critic Paul Morley and handcuffing himself to his host Jonathan Ross on live television in a wretched parody of the 70s Bill Grundy interview with the Sex Pistols, entitled his polemic, "Why Should Having Fun Be Against The Law?" He voiced the opinion that:

> Britain is already vastly over-regulated. The Government should pursue a truly Thatcherite course and deregulate night club licensing. If normal night clubs were allowed to open until all hours the demand for warehouse parties would decline. Surely this ridiculous 3 a.m. curfew on dancing is an anachronism in today's enterprise culture.

Less surprisingly perhaps, the *New Musical Express* (*NME*, February 10, 1990) sympathetically presented a "Freedom to Party" rally in Trafalgar Square at the beginning of 1990 as (responsibly) arguing against "drug taking" and as being explicitly in favour of an extension of "legal venues" as "the way forward" and "looking for nightclub licensing to be extended to six or eight in the morning" (or even encouraging England to follow the Scottish example of 5 a.m. licensing).

There are several strands of the historical origins of the development of the media narrative of Acid House/rave culture which are significant. Not all of them have been pursued in this Chapter - others are taken up in various Chapters in this book - but one is the line that can be drawn from the early 80s warehouse parties which grew, eventually, from an illegal underground to a general reflection of 'enterprise culture' by the early 90s. Although this period coincided with the 'Thatcher years' it is not so much that a free market ideology was pursued as such. However, the right to *organise* parties displaced the right simply to party in the "Freedom to Party" pressure group politics. Moreover, the acceptance of the profit-making motive in the organisation of such events drew widespread support from punters, especially in the wake of an increasing state moral authoritarianism and constant media tales of youth in T-shirts being met by police in riot gear at many raves.

The Ecstasy of politics?

Previous theorists of post-war popular music, youth culture and deviance (whether from Cultural Studies or Radical, or New, Deviancy Theory traditions) have tended to look beneath or behind, the surfaces of the shimmering media-scape in order to discover the 'real', authentic subculture, apparently always distorted by the manufactured press and television image, which in turn becomes 'real' as more and more participants act out the media stereotypes. This 'depth model' is no longer appropriate - indeed if it ever were - to analyse the surfaces of (post) modern culture, a culture characterised by depthlessness, flatness and 'hyperreality' as Jean Baudrillard has labelled it. Whether Baudrillard's notions of media saturated self-referential culture can have any analytical purchase on studies of youth culture is examined in later Chapters of this book. Nevertheless, one difficulty with applying the subcultural method to the Acid House/rave phenomenon is that what is thrown up by such an archaeology is the debris of 'scally' culture, a label universally applied in the late 80s to the youthful wearing of flares and other baggy attire in any city or town north of Watford - especially Manchester. Despite the quite distinct origins of Perries (originally Fred Perry Boys) in Manchester and Scallies in Liverpool in the late 70s on the soccer terraces, and in the music clubs of these and other cities, the universal application of scally to a 'young thief in the right training shoes' during the 80s and early 90s obscures a long and complex history of a casual youth style which is impervious to analysis with the aid of the orthodox tools of contemporary subcultural theory. For youth subcultures prior to the early 70s, there was generally held to be an authenticity about their street-generated style. Thus, teds, beats, rockers, mods, skins, hippies, rudies and Rastas sustained an explosion of literature about them, which largely applauded them for their much-flaunted signs of resistance and rebellion towards contemporary society, and which frequently ignored *both* their overt machismo and the regular association - from teddy boys onwards - of subcultures and gay culture which

23

often involves a subversion of traditional notions of masculinity. After 1970, however, manufactured subcultures were constantly spotted as first Glam (Bowie, T. Rex, Gary Glitter) and later disco took over the night time economy of many cities and towns. Punk was always going to be a hybrid of manufacture/authenticity, explaining the rigorous debate which has raged ever since about the subculture's origins in the art school or dole queue. Whatever the accuracy of the various positions in this argument, post-punk subcultures have been characterised by a speeding up of the time between points of authenticity and manufacture. 'Acid House' is a particularly good example of this; as Neville Wakefield notes about the months after the 'Summer of Love' 88!

> ...what we witnessed over the course of the year was an accelerating closure of the gap between the original and its retrosurrection....The emergence of Acid House as a discernible musical genre in the spring of 1988 completed the ever-decreasing circle of revivalism...and imploded the past into a permanent (and danceable) present". (14)

The problem for pop and youth culture history is that if subcultural explanations (of Ecstasy use, (15) for instance) can now finally be laid to rest, their contemporary irrelevance throws into the melting pot the accepted theories and histories of the connections between pop, youth and deviance *before* the 1980s as well as after.

Notes

1. See, in particular, the continuing ethnographic work *A Sociological Investigation Concerning the Relationship Between Knowledge and Experience involving the use of the Drug MDMA,* by Alan Haughton, Research Assistant in the Unit for Law and Popular Culture, 1990-92. This, to our knowledge, is the first ethnography of Ecstasy use in Britain, exploring the different accounts given of Ecstasy and working closely with users. This chapter is indebted to Alan Haughton's research work.

2. The scope of this work extends to a study of the regulation of youth culture in the day and night-time economies of regions such as Greater Manchester; see Derek Wynne, Steve Redhead, Justin O'Connor, et al: *The Culture Industry*, (1992, Gower, Aldershot) and Steve Redhead, *Unpopular Cultures,* (Manchester University Press, Manchester, forthcoming). See also the theoretical work in Steve Redhead, *The End of the Century Party: Youth and Pop Towards 2000,* (1990), Manchester University Press, Manchester.

3. *Raving and Dance Drugs,* (1990) paper on house music clubs and parties in North West England, available from the author, Russell Newcombe.

4. A. Fraser, L. Gamble and P. Kennet *Into The Pleasuredrome,* (1991).

5. Mark Gilman, 'Everything Starts With An E', in *Druglink,* November/December, 1991.

6. *Folk Devils and Moral Panics,* (1990), Blackwell, Oxford.

7. The last quotation is from Sarah Champion, *And God Created Manchester,* (1990), Wordsmith, Manchester. The others in this section were compiled by Alan Haughton in his research into Ecstasy users in Manchester 1990-92.

8. However, some of the countries in the New Europe are

following Manchester's example of crackdown. *The Guardian,* of June 7, 1991, reported that "Italy's dance culture is fighting a decree for 2 a.m. closing" despite - as in Manchester - dance culture being a major leisure and tourist industry. Government sources cited fighting and noise among crowds emerging from discos at first light as the reasons for the decree. For some of the problems associated with the British government's legal onslaught on dance culture, especially changes brought about by the campaign for and against the Entertainment (Increased Penalties) Act, 1990, see Steve Redhead, Rave Off: Youth, Subculture and The Law, in *Social Studies Review,* Vol. 6, No. 3, 1991. See also Jon Savage (ed.), *The Haçienda Must Be Built,* (1992), International Music Publications, London.

9. For an account of one such trip see Steve Redhead and Justin O'Connor, 'Popular Culture in Paris and Manchester', *Bop City,* 2, May 1990.

10. Drug related gang rivalry also exists *within* Moss Side, particularly involving the Gooch Close gang and the Pepperhill (after a local pub, The Pepperhill) mob; see 'Drug Gangs wage war for control of Moss Side', in *The Observer,* May 5, 1991.

11. For the most sober - and sobering - account of the escalation (in the media) of stories of gang warfare in Manchester, see Ian Taylor, *Fear and Loathing in Greater Manchester,* Department of Sociology, University of Salford, April, 1991.

12. See Jay Stevens, *Storming Heaven: LSD And The American Dream,* (1988), Heinemann, London, especially pages 373-374, on the decision by the Drug Enforcement Agency to place Ecstasy on Schedule 1, which meant that manufacturing or selling the drug would be punishable by a possible fine of $125,000 and fifteen years in prison.

13. See Mark Heley, 'High Time to Get Smart', in *The Guardian,* June 8, 1991.

14. Neville Wakefield, *Postmodernism: The Twilight of the Real,* (1990), Pluto Press, London, p. 10.

15. This chapter has its origins in a conference on *Drugs in Democratic Societies* organised in June, 1991, by the Association Descartes in Paris. I am particularly grateful to Patrick Mignon and his colleagues for inviting me and the helpful critical comments I received from the audience in Paris.

3 The ecstasy of disappearance

Antonio Melechi

As has been analysed elsewhere (Melechi and Redhead, 1988) in the autumn of 1988 Acid House was exposed to the glaring visibility of a national tabloid campaign. *The Sun* captained an offensive of panic proportions, revealing the sordid truth behind the cult that they had at the beginning of October greeted as "cool and groovy". In this panic the culture's own 'Summer of Love' (the re-working of another mythical summer) was transformed into a sex and drugs nightmare, where 'Acid Mr. Bigs' sucked the innocent into a hellish nightmare, and the media blitz spawned a police crack-down on Acid House parties held in disused warehouses around the country.

While the 'eye' of police power sought to cast its gaze over these previously neglected spaces, the pop chroniclers played detectives investigating the origins of the phenomenon, tracing the stolen signifiers of this subcultural style: Acid (LSD), Ecstasy (amphetamine based stimulant), tacky beachwear, psychedelia, sampled sounds, Lucozade, Smiley badges/logos and fluorescent accessories. Tracing this catalogue of plundering back to its rightful sources Acid House was given sensible shape: pop critic Stuart Cosgrove (1988) could see subcultural history repeated; the Ecstasy drug scare mirrored the media response to amphetamines and the mods in the mid-60s. Similarly, DJ Mark Moore of S-Express could argue that "it's the same reaction old fogies had when rock 'n' roll first started" (quoted in Roberts, 1988), and even *The Sunday Times* could chip in with their own piece of nostalgia:

If they had been born 10 years earlier they would have been punk rockers and sniffed glue, if they had been born 20 years earlier taken LSD and listened to Jim Morrison. (Prangnell, 1988).

Acid House: alternatively punk, rock 'n' roll, and hippy revival, consistently refracted through a subcultural mythology which it was seen to appropriate and reiterate. Pop analysts failed to theorise the actual origins of Acid House in the contemporary space in which it was born, at the zero degree of popular culture: the package holiday. It is here in the definitively postmodern experience of self, that the British phenomenon of Acid House belongs, attempting to relive the jouissance of the Mediterranean holiday in the pleasures of dance, music and drugs.

Tourism, as a subject of serious study, remains a generally neglected area. If we are looking to frame the subcultural beginnings of Acid House, 1,500 miles from Britain in the Balearic island of Ibiza, the concept of the 'tourist gaze' provides one of the few attempts to theorise the world of popular travel and holidays: "What makes a particular form of tourist gaze depends upon what it is contrasted with, what the forms of non-tourist experience happen to be." (Urry, 1992, p.2).

In seeking to apply this approach in an understanding of the small group of holidaymakers in Ibiza town (the original 'acid ravers') the concept of the tourist gaze is limited. In the context of Acid House it is not only the difference between 'home' and 'away' which defines the gaze, but also the contrast with another holiday experience: the movement from the original destination of San Antonio:

> The northwest town of San Antonio, with its British pubs and fish and chip shops, was a soul weekender nightmare. Ibiza Town on the other hand was the playground of the rich and famous, boasting fantasy discotheques and a haven from animal antics....In 85/86 the young UK clubber, seeking refuge from San Antonio, started to join them partying on a cocktail of sun, Ecstasy and mixture of records only a Mediterranean island could get away with. (Godfrey, 1990).

The resort of San Antonio welcomed incoming arrivals with a self contained pocket of domestic culture, a home from home, where the British holidaymaker could take a full English breakfast at the Hotel Pueblo, watch Top Gun in the TV lounge, bump into friends at the

Rocky Horror Game Show and dance to the top twenty at Cinderella Rockerfellers. Signs of an indigenous population or culture were few and the British tourist intent on 'going native' would make do with paella and sangria. For those who sought to escape this imperial exercise in bad taste, and stray beyond the brochure to Ibiza Town, at the other side of the island, there was something else: a more upmarket resort, away from the drone of familiar accents and the banality of the burger bar, where the tourist could enjoy the pleasure of anonymity whilst settling into the twelve hour cycle of clubbing at Pasha, Amnesia, Glory's and Manhattan's. The club scene at Ibiza town, on the other side of the island, would in this way become the stomping ground for a small group of metropolitan 'ravers', who would return annually to spend the summer together. If the resort provided possibilities that were unrealised at San Antonio, these had been equally unavailable in British clubs. The difference between Britain and Ibiza (the tourist gaze) is clearly expressed by DJ Alfredo, an Argentine who spent six years at Ibiza's famous Amnesia:

> I've always considered Britain to be the most creative country musically...you are also very good at packaging and labelling things, this I don't like so much. It's all part of the island mentality, you look inwards....At the club I was always used to mixing up good sound from all over Europe....I play a mixture of sounds as always, fuck them all, I never say never to anything. The mixture of backgrounds in Ibiza opens up all possibilities (quoted in Godfrey, 1990).

While the British club scene, based on predominantly domestic sounds, organised its market around specific musical forms and subcultural identities (rap, house, jazz, soul, etc.) these distinctions were collapsed in the heterogeneity of the 'Balearic Beat', where the eclectic mishmash of Peter Gabriel, Public Enemy, Jibaro and the Woodentops would be fused together. However, while these difference between respective club cultures are significant, they are in many ways peripheral to the experience of the tourist subculture that would adopt Ibiza as its twin town. To formulate the tourist gaze in this fashion is liable to turn the holidaymaker into an anthropologist, reflexively absorbing and adopting the rituals of an alien lifestyle. While this approach makes some sense of hippy trailers, round-the-worlders and holidaymakers bound for Paris, Florence and Madrid, this is a distinct order of tourist in search of culture, history and spectacle. The Ibizan reveller high on Ecstasy, abandoned to the beat, lost under the strobe lights consumes the radically different space of Dionysian pleasure: dance, music and drugs. To understand the pleasures of the dance floor we must move to a different logic of tourism where one comes to hide from the spectre of a former self (Britain and San Antonio) to disaccumulate culture and disappear under the dry ice and into the body. This is the jouissance of Amnesia, where nobody is but everybody belongs.

The postmodern experience of cultural disaccumulation finds its perfect expression in Jean Baudrillard's America, where the relation between Europe and its transatlantic other provides a paradigm for that between Britain and Ibiza Town in the birth of Acid House:

> In reality you do not, as I had hoped, get any distance on Europe from here. You do not acquire a fresh angle on it. When you turn round, it has quite simply disappeared. The point is that there is really no need to adopt a critical stance on Europe from here...what you have to do is enter the fiction of America (p.29).

For Baudrillard, America is hyperreal, a dazzling surface where Marineworld, Disneyland and Hearst's Castle serve only to perpetuate the myth of the real: Cape Canaveral, the White House and the rest of America. Baudrillard claims that the "real is no longer real" in America, the principle of simulation has taken over, manically secreting signs of the real. There is no depth, truth, meaning or identity here. In America everything is simply just as it appears.

Ibiza Town's world of fantasy discotheques offers a subculture the same possibilities as the American hyperreal does Baudrillard: a cultural void, a seductive absence and enticing void where one can partake in the ecstasy of disappearance. Baudrillard approaches America as a national holiday complex, wallowing in the emptiness and banality, cruising the highways and scanning the panoply of consumer objects. Baudrillard cares little for the social and historical, he has come to chill out. There is only one question he asks of his journey: "How far can we go into the extermination of meaning?" (p.10).

Tourism, in both cases, amounts to a pleasurable psychosis as the holidaymaker submits to the loss of cultural and self identity. The nature of the tourist gaze in this way frames a postmodern subjectivity: the unthinkable alterity of pure indifference which the tourist encounters is that between the meaningful and the meaningless, the real and the imaginary. It is the dance floor which represents the magical surface where a small group of metropolitan tourists would become urban shamans pushing the bounds of holiday anonymity into this ritual of disappearance.

Acid House would be born of this nostalgia, and by the end of the summer of '87 holiday-sick clubbers arrived back home in London intent on resurrecting the spirit of Ibiza Town. In November, the Shoom Club opened its doors to a crowd of conspicuous ex-tourists dressed in a colourful array of shorts, T-shirts and bandanas, with the newly adopted Smiley logo conferring (at this time) secret subcultural membership.

The re-staging of Balearic memories over metropolitan weekends would rely, more than ever, on the spell of the dance floor to effect the disappearing act that had been previously aided by the hyperreality of tourism and Ibiza Town. The pleasures of loss and abandonment would now be purely signalled by the 'trance-dance', as the body would plug into a qualitatively different space from that of dance in pop history.

From jiving to break dancing the body has been traditionally structured by the (male) gaze grounding the meaning of dance as exhibition. A different sense of dance in Acid House is suggested by Jenny Rampling of the Shoom Club: "people come 'cos they can totally relax and freak out as much as they want without anybody standing and watching them". (Quoted in Godfrey, 1988). The same sentiment is reiterated in the lyrics of the song 'Trance-Dance' by D-Mob:

> Now this dance it started in the discos, where we all go, when everybody comes down and not to frown. For those who come to pose they get into their nose, 'cos they're dancing - trance-dancing....To the trance-dance...not to romance.

In this way the trance-dance moves the body beyond the spectacle of the 'pose' and the sexuality ('romance') of the look, into a 'cyber-space' of musical sound, where one attempts to implode (get into) and disappear. It is a transition which, in a more general sense, is anticipated by Baudrillard in his essay on the *Ecstasy of Communication*, (published by Semiotext(e)):

> The hot, sexual obscenity [of former time] is followed by cool communicational obscenity....[the cold and communicational, contractual and motivational obscenity of today]. The former [clearly] implied a type of promiscuity...[unlike this] organic, visceral, carnal [promiscuity]...while the promiscuity which reigns over the communication networks is one of superficial saturation ...[the pleasure is no longer one of manifestation, scenic and aesthetic, but rather one] of pure fascination, aleatory and psychotropic.

The articulation of a new space of the non-spectacle in Acid House where the body is neither the subject of self-expression nor the object of the gaze, is effected in the space of the sound which the dancer attempts to 'get into'. An electronic soundtrack of sampled sound, a collage of woven fragments, is underscored by a hypnotically insistent beat which provides the bottom line for the body: the minimal 'information' required for the dancer to be consumed in the 'communication'. Acid House music is based on the absence of an originary subject, the 'soul' of pop discourse, as the presence of a founding voice is sacrificed into a digitally complex wall of reconstituted sound. To adapt McLuhan's terminology we have both the 'hotting' up of the message in this dense accumulation of heterogeneous data and a fundamental transformation in the medium (and message) in the new technology of 'inhuman functionalism' - sampling.

Following McLuhan's thesis that changes in the medium have 'social and personal consequences' it can be said that these are directly discernible through the collapse of the traditional field of spectacle and expression in pop, where the 'user' sought self-expression through dance. Acid House celebrates the death of this *scene* of dance, for it is now the materiality of the musical signifier which forms the new space of oblivion, as the dancer implodes and disappears into a technological dreamscape of sound.

If, as Hebdige suggests (1988, p.35), the politics of youth since the 50s have been principally enacted through a spectacle of style and body, the invisibility which the Acid House subculture has attempted to attain (by escaping traditional sites of surveillance and mapping a

34

new sphere of sound) moves to a new order of politics and resistance. The specific implications of this displacement are most obvious in the field of the sexual, for as Luce Irigaray argues the concept of sexual difference, in a tradition of Western thought, has been located at the level of the gaze: the phallic domain of visibility where female absence is reflected. Acid House's spectacle of disappearance, beyond the gaze, targets the indifferent body as the object of consumption. The subcultural tradition of sex, desire and romance has moved to a different plane of pleasures as the combination of dance, music and Ecstasy slides the body into an amphetamine bliss and the jouissance of cyber-space.

As the national tabloid campaign switched the lights on the Acid House party, the subcultural phenomenon was to be subjected to a hysterical re-inscription in the traditional logic of spectacle and difference:

> Police raided a huge Acid House disco yesterday - then fled to let 3,000 teenagers carry on raving it up at the sex and drugs orgy....*Sun* reporters saw PUSHERS openly selling Ecstasy, a drug which heightens sexual awareness, but can lead to hallucinations and heart attacks...OUTRAGEOUS sex romps taking place on a special stage in front of the dance floor (*The Sun*, November 7, 1988).

The Acid House story was duly re-written in a tabloid version of the bogeyman (combining the moralism of the cautionary tale with the excess of the horror story) as acid pied pipers sought to seduce their unsuspecting prey (typically young girls) with their evil wares, calling on the alluring spell of 'killer music' and the hypnotic charm of their sinister calling cards: Smiley. This spectacle of sexualization in the media narrative was to reach its perfect expression with *The Sun* leader: "Acid Fiends Spike Page Three Girl's Drink" (November 24, 1988), and the story of Tracy Kirkby's attempted rape by 'evil Spaniards'.

By late 88 Radio 1 had banned Acid House, Smiley had sold out to the high street, and youth magazines and clubzines derided 'Acid Teds' who discovered the subculture as it became mainstream. In subcultural terms Acid House had, by the end of 88, died a death, but the clubbers that had originally championed it were alive and kicking. Despite the stepping up of police surveillance on clubs, service stations and possible illegal venues, the use of Ecstasy was rapidly increasing and rave organisers showed greater enterprise in securing aircraft hangars, derelict churches, caves and a variety of unlikely locations for illegal parties.

Into 1989 the rave scene began to attract an increasingly wider audience. While club culture purists insist that 88 was the one and only 'Summer of Love', it was, in many ways, merely an inkling of what was to happen in 89, as raves became a crossroads where unlikely subcultures (football, Indie and traveller, amongst others) would meet. Ecstasy was undoubtedly the catalyst of this coming together.

The death of Acid House marked a momentous transformation in youth and club culture. From the pleasures of implosion and disappearance, a new atmosphere of sociability began to emerge, a sense of community which manifested itself in new revivals of contact (hugging, kissing and massaging) and exchange (drinks, joints, cigarettes and poppers). DJs now turned towards more melodic and soulful forms of house music - deep, Italian and garage. If club culture had before celebrated an ecstasy of selflessness and oblivion, the new ecstasy was one of belonging and togetherness, of brothers and sisters in a 'Promised Land'.

With the introduction of the Entertainment (Increased Penalties) Act (dubbed the Acid House Bill) in 1990 - securing even greater power for the policing of Britain's night life - domestic club culture increasingly looked to European clubs for its 'Promised Land'. The new found popularity of Italian house, initially championed by DJs like Danny Rampling and Kid Batchelor, sparked an unprecedented interest in the Italian club scene. With many clubbers looking for an alternative to Ibiza, the last two years have seen Rimini - Italy's clubbing capital - develop into a popular holiday destination.

Christened Italy's Las Vegas by Umberto Eco, Rimini is a resort built entirely around its nightlife and is the home of the biggest and glitziest discotheques in Europe. The biggest of the Riviera clubs, the Baie Imperiale - a mock homage to antiquity, and one-time film set for Cleopatra - has a capacity of 10,000. Pascia and Cocorico, two of the Riviera's trendiest clubs, are respectively styled as an oriental palace and a gigantic glass pyramid. Clubland on the Riviera is a series of extravagant follies, a kitsch celebration of excess.

Yet, despite its spectacular club scene, Rimini, unlike Ibiza, is not home to a subculture, it is pure consumerism. The image of Rimini as a den of iniquity and transgression is one promoted by artistic directors at the Riveria's clubs, and hyped in magazines like Discotec and Tuttodisco. The outrageous starlets that can be spotted in Rimini's clubs, parading in bondage and drag, squirming in giant platters of spaghetti, are merely part of the floor show, unlike Britain and Ibiza where clubbers are stars of their own show.

Summer weekends in Italy see an exodus of Italian youngsters - a process dubbed 'Saturday Night Fever' by the media - who converge on the Riviera in convoy. At the beginning of 1990 the press began to focus on the phenomenon, with weekly reports on its accidents and casualties. The ensuing response to 'Saturday Night Fever' reveals one essential difference in the policing of youth culture in Britain and Italy. While the tabloid reaction to Acid House precipitated an essentially legal response in Britain, the moral panic in Italy was primarily familial - headed by a group of parents nicknamed 'Le mamme anti-rock'.

For the pop critics, club culture's 'ravers' and 'revellers' confirmed the death of youth culture. This was a 'bleak generation' lost in a world of bacchanalian pleasures. The old language of resistance, empowerment and identity, which had claimed a long line of folk devils as the return of the repressed, was redundant in the face of a subculture whose rank and file were socially diverse. The more general problems for critics who would attempt to *read* youth and club culture, was the emergence of a scene without stars and spectacle, gaze and identification. Those who sought to understand this subculture in terms of a politics of usage and identity completely missed the point, the spaces which club culture occupied and transformed through Ecstasy and travel (retreating into the body, holidaying in Ibiza and Rimini) represent a fantasy of liberation, an escape from identity. A place where nobody is, but everybody belongs.

The recuperation of Acid House in the gaze of police surveillance and tabloid discourse leads us on to questions of resistance which have, in one form or another, typically framed subcultural formations. The limited analysis which Acid House has received has generally approached these 'ravers' and 'revellers' as deserters of the subcultural cause lost in the unsocial world of bacchanalian pleasures. When Stuart Cosgrove (1988) argues that Acid House "pleasures come not from resistance but from surrender" it is clear that the new logic of subcultural response evades the easy opposition between surrender and resistance. While subcultural refusals have been traditionally effected through the statement of self-expression and the display of alternative identity, Acid House has relinquished this ground and returns to the experience of tourism, where the self is lost in the 'unculture of the hyperreal'. This strategy of resistance to the scene of identity necessitates an escape from the (media) gaze, as, unlike previous subcultures which remain "hiding in the light" (Hebdige, 1988, p.35), a whole subculture attempts to vanish. This mode of disappearance is complex and contradictory, for as Baudrillard notes in analysing the effects of the media:

> ...the individual is not only condemned to disappearance, but it is also a strategy, it is a way of response to this device for capture, for networking, and for forced identification.

This is the enigmatic void of Acid House: where the invisible hide and the mute prefer silence, where the ecstasy of disappearance resists the imperative to reveal one's self.

Bibliography

Barnes, G. (1988) 'Acid House Kids Lured to Holland', *Daily Mirror,* 14/11/92.

Baudrillard, J. (1988) *America,* translated by C. Turner.   Verso, London.

Baudrillard, J. (1987) *The Ecstasy of Communication,* published by Semiotext(e) Foreign Agents Series, (1988), Automedia, New York.

Cosgrove, S. (1988) 'Forbidden Fruits', *New Statesman and Society,* September 2.

Godfrey, J. (1988) 'The Amnesiacs', *The Independent,* June.

Godfrey, J. (1988) 'Club Column', *The Independent,* September.

Godfrey, J. and Collin, M. (eds) (1990) 'Playpen', *The Independent,* April.

Grossberg, L. (1984) 'I'd Rather Feel Bad Than Not Feel Anything At All', *Enclictic,* No. 8, pp. 94-111.

Grossberg, L. (1984) 'Rock and Roll: Pleasure and Power', (Op cit. pp. 94-111).

Hebdige, D. (1988) *Hiding in the Light: On Images and Things,* Comedia, London.

Kay, J. (1988) 'Acid Fiends Spike Page Three Girls Drink', *The Sun,* November 24.

Melechi, A. and Redhead, S. (1988) 'The Fall of the Acid Reign', *New Statesman and Society,* December 23.

Prangnell, M. (1988) 'The Summer of Acid House Hype', *The Sunday Times Review,* October 31.

Roberts, D. (1988) 'The Grin Factor', *Q,* October.

Urry, J. (1990) *The Tourist Gaze* , Sage, London.

Willis, P. and Fielder, M. (1988) 'Acid Rain Cops Flee 3,000 At Party', *The Sun* , November 7.

Wood, H. (1988) '£12 Trip to Evil Night of Ecstacy', *Daily Mirror*, November 7.

4 Living the dream

Hillegonda Rietveld

The rave as event

> We can wear ourselves out in materialising things, in rendering them visible, but we will never cancel the secret.... Even the protagonists of the secret would not know how to betray it, because it is no more than a ritual act of complicity, a sharing of the absence of truth and appearances.
> Jean Baudrillard, 1987.[1]

Since 1988 the press, from tabloid to subcultural, has made the attempt to reveal the spectacle of the 'Acid House cult' and its event, the rave. Young people with bandanas, brightly coloured clothes and a crazed look in their eyes were presented as the next youth subculture. Subsequently, certain stereotypes in behaviour and dress sense were identified. In the meantime, ravers of the multitude of clubs, blues parties, warehouses and festivals abandoned themselves to a ritual of disappearance.

The rave is a dance party, where the music has its origins in Acid House from Chicago, techno from Detroit and garage from New York, which themselves had evolved from dance-musical styles that were played in mainly (black) gay clubs, especially The Warehouse in Chicago and Paradise Garage in New York. House music had already gained a place of prominence in Manchester during 1986-87.

Apart from the music, the formalist aspects of these parties (the extensive use of strobe lights, dry ice and psychedelic imagery) seem to be derived from the Acid Test parties in California of the 1960s.(2) These were revived during the winter of 1987, together with Ibiza inspired holiday clothes and a Balearic 'mishmash' of musical styles, in London clubs like Shoom and Future. In 1988 this resulted in what seemed like a repeat of the 'Summer of Love', first in London and later in other parts of the country. At the end of that summer, rave parties started to occur outside of the regulated club environment, like in abandoned industrial spaces and open fields. The participants of the rave do not drink alcohol but take mainly the illegal drug MDMA or Ecstasy ('E') as a recreational intoxicant. This is a type of amphetamine which has empathic effects: social inhibitions and the need for private space are drastically reduced.(3) In this frenzied and yet relaxed atmosphere, a do-what-you-like dress code developed with initially a baggy appearance.

Taking into account the panic reaction of the 'establishment' as the cult took hold of the nation's imagination, one might suspect that a new counter-culture had arrived. This Chapter will therefore ask whether this is indeed the case and if not, what could be its precise place on the cultural 'map' of Britain? For this purpose, a canon of current cultural theory with a post-structuralist edge will be excavated. As the narrative (which describes the period of 1988-90) unfolds, an attempt will be made to reveal some of the historical roots of the rave.

The method employed is to look at different representations of the rave. The main sources of information for the research have been books, magazines, academic articles, the tabloid press and 'quality' newspapers with related interests, as well as interviews with participants involved in production as well as consumption. In addition, extensive practical participant observation research of rave-events in the North West of England was undertaken.

First, the essay gives an account of the reaction of the establishment to the rave (called 'Acid House Party' in the discourse of the mass-media of 1988-90) and the subsequent making of the 'Acid Test' in 1990. In the autumn of 1988 the tabloid press started to create an image of 'Acid House' and its cultural trappings as that of gendered and sexualised evil.(4) This reveals less about the rave than about the contemporary social order itself. There seemed to be an eagerness to cleanse the consciousness of the 'darker' side of the

Thatcherite entrepreneurial spirit of the 80s. As a result of this type of publicity, rave events became big business, as though constituting a self-fulfulling prophecy.(5) Major police interference in the form of raids and harassment eventually accumulated into the criminalisation of the Acid House or rave, i.e. more people, who were previously law-abiding, were defined as behaving in a criminal manner. On the other hand criminal elements, who did not mind making a profit from breaking the law, started to get themselves involved. In the end a back bench Conservative MP, Graham Bright, stepped in and introduced the Entertainments (Increased Penalties) Bill, which became law in the summer of 1990.

The chroniclers of pop pointed out that this was nothing really new. Moral panics have occurred before in reaction to subcultures of (usually working class) youth, which is often defined as a repressed category in society. As with teddy boys, rockers, hippies, Rastas, mods, skins or punks in the past, a resistance through style was suspected. According to Dick Hebdige, young people pose in order to "pose a threat", to "challenge the symbolic order which guarantees their subordination".(6) Their visual style is the expression of resistance. The raver was seen to enter the world of consumerism, in order to keep ahead of the recuperation of its own 'secret' signs. In this way, youth subcultures seem to develop like eternal cycles of resistance, recuperation and a new resistance.(7) Alternatively, theoreticians of the 'postmodern' painted a picture of pure (i.e. 'meaningless') appearances. The stolen signs of a first mythical 'Summer of Love', which occurred in 1967, were seen to be nostalgically retraced. It seems doubtful that a critical distance in these times of rapid communication can be maintained. It may even be impossible to enter the eternal circle of resistance and recuperation; instead a counter-cultural inertia (although using the signs of a counter-culture) could be identified.

It is therefore possible to argue, that a (political) critique was never posed. Rather, a threat to the symbolic order was made by the attempt to avoid it altogether. No meaning could be found other than pure escape, suggesting, perhaps, a type of tourism.(8) There was the excitement of spending money that had lost its exchange value and of driving into the darkness, the unknown. A disappearance from daily material realities by an undoing of the constructed 'self' in a Dionysian(9) ritual is the ultimate effect. "Let the music take control"(10) now enter the Living Dream (in three versions of representation) where "everything starts with an E" (11).

Sources

1. Jean Baudrillard, *The Ecstasy of Communication*, (1988), Semiotext(e), pp. 64-65.

2. Tom Wolfe, *The Electric Kool-Aid Acid Test*, (1989), Black Swan.

3. Jay Stevens, *Storming Heaven: LSD and the American Dream*, (1989), Paladin, p.487.

4. Steve Redhead and Antonio Melechi, 'The Fall of the Acid Reign', *New Statesman and Society,* 23/30 December, 1988.

5. Edward W. Said, *Orientalism,* (1985), Peregrine Books, p.94.

6. Dick Hebdige, *Hiding in the Light,* (1988), Comedia, 1988, p.18.

7. Dick Hebdige, *Subculture: The Meaning of Style,* (1979), Methuen, p.100.

8. Antonio Melechi, *The Ecstasy of Disappearance,* Chapter 3 in this publication.

9. Friedrich Nietschze, *The Birth of Tragedy,* (1871), Anchor, 1956, p.22.

10. Anambi, *Burning up inside,* (1991), Robs Records.

11. E-Zee Possee, *Everything Starts with an E,* (1988), More Protein, Virgin Records.

Entrepreneurs

There is a rather complex dialectic of reinforcement by which the experiences of readers in reality are determined by what they have read, and this in turn influences writers to take up subjects defined in advance by readers' experiences...we might expect that the ways it is recommended that a lion's fierceness be handled will actually increase its fierceness, force it to be fierce since that is what it is, and that is what in essence we know or can ONLY know about it.
Edward W. Said (1978).(1)

...it is precisely as a 'scandal' that the other is structurally necessary, for it defines the limits of the bourgeois social text - what is (a)social, (ab)normal, (sub)cultural.
Hal Foster (1985).(2)

At the end of the summer of 1988 the tabloid press identified a new form of entertainment for contemporary youth, the rave, which they labelled as 'Acid House'. The latter was a type of music played in clubs and warehouse-parties, which somehow seemed to turn its 'punters' into a state of raving frenzy. Sun-tanned people with grins on their faces were spotted wearing brightly coloured Mediterranean holiday clothes and details that gave the 'look' a slight 1960s hippy accent. The Smiley insignia was identified as their 'secret' icon. On October 1, *The Sun* called it "cool and groovy", but soon the headlines changed. Redhead and Melechi identified in the press the construction of "Acid Pied Pipers, the 'Mister Bigs' of Acid House - unscrupulous drug dealers and warehouse party organisers...in a seduction of the innocent".(3) *The Sun* spoke of the "Evil of Ecstasy" (October 19). *The Post* shouted "Ban this Killer Music" (October 24). The next day *The Sun* topped this up with "Acid House Horror", followed three days later with "Drug Crazed Acid House Fans" and culminating at the end of the month with "Girl 21 Drops Dead At Acid Disco".

Redhead and Melechi argue that the portrayal of the victims of this 'evil cult' quickly shifted from the category of young people in general to specifically the 'young woman'. Young girls were spotted smoking cannabis or taking the hallucinogenic drug LSD. The amphetamine designer drug Ecstasy, the drug that has been closely related to Acid

House events, was described as a 'sex drug'. The danger of sexual violation was implied. This was made explicit when on November 24, *The Sun* ran the headline "Acid Fiends Spike Page Three Girl's Drink", with the intention of rape, as the article explained.(4)

Acid House seemed good material for an exaggerated reiteration of the myth of Sex, Drugs and Rock & Roll. People were shocked and 'titillated'. In the summer and autumn of 1988 the mass media gave attention to something that before had been just good dancing parties. Youngsters were alerted: they wanted in on the action. And so did the money grabbers, like local gangs, euphemistically called Firms. And so did the subculturalists. An escalation of activity around the Acid House phenomenon was the result of this discourse, an example of which is a tabloid article on November 7, when The Sun reported of "3,000 At Party, Drug Pushers Carry On" at "the sex-and-drugs orgy".(5)

Over the winter of 1988-9 the exaggerated myth making of events calmed down in the public eye. Many rave events had been forced out of the city centres due to unwanted attention by the local police and civic establishment. For a short while dance parties had become invisible in suburban terrain on locations such as disused industrial spaces. Occasionally there were front-page warnings, like the "The Acid Houses of Death" which symbolised fire hazards as ravers blocked fire exits in order to prevent the police from entering the party premises.(6) In June 1989 however, the tabloids announced that "11,000 youngsters go drug crazy at Britain's biggest-ever Acid Party", the party organised by the Sunrise organisation in an aircraft hangar, illustrated with a photograph of a bunch of wildly gesturing ravers.(7) Youth was yet again pointed out as a source of trouble. The 'Acid Baron' popped up his ugly head too. And there were more victims: "Tragedy of acid house drug girl, 16", announced the *Manchester Evening News* in the middle of July 1989, when a teenage girl died after having taken the drug Ecstasy in a Manchester club, the Haçienda.(8)

According to Heley and Collin, 89's "warehouse events...have roots in a culture of illegal parties which began in 1978 and 1979 with three warehouse parties in...South London".(9) On the other hand there have been Blues Parties within the West Indian community for the last 30 or 40 years. The latter inspired a place like The Kitchen in Hulme, Manchester: an all week party which did not charge any entry fee. The main reason for organising these events seems to be the fact that in England clubs generally close at 2 or 3 a.m. As Tony Colston-Hayter put it, "Surely this ridiculous 3 a.m. curfew on dancing is an anachronism in today's enterprise culture".(10)   A certain amount of enterprise was involved in the organisation of all of these events. The big rave events that finally survived the summer of 1989 were professionally organised with profit in mind in true Thatcherite spirit.   The problem however, was that freedom of enterprise in the strictest sense means no interference by the government. Party organisers took this idea of liberty to their hearts with more zeal than was expected of the average citizen. Although often enough venues were checked for fire hazards by the fire brigade, there were problems with uncollected tax and a black market in consumer paraphernalia such as illegal stimulants and hallucinogenic drugs. The Acid House entrepreneur as 'folk devil' took hold of the public imagination.

The police stepped up their action. Kent police established a special squad to trace the organisation of parties in Kent and its surrounding counties in order to prevent their occurrence. Elsewhere in the country the police initially showed a relatively tolerant attitude. For example, in March 1989, there was a party in a church building in Huddersfield.   The premises were entered at the end of its legal rental time by a 25 strong police force, while it had been surrounded and kept under surveillance all night, they were generally friendly and polite. However, by the end of the summer, a contradiction in policies became apparent. The open air extravaganza Joy, near Rochdale, was officially policed; this was paid for by the party organisation, as happens with any other large public event that can cause traffic and parking problems. At the same time there were court injunctions served on the more well known DJs preventing them from entering Rochdale and its surrounding area on the particular weekend of the event. The injunction, plus stories of police 'busts' of parties elsewhere earlier on in the summer, discouraged many ravers from trying to get there.

Less radical advocates of free enterprise within the Conservative government, representatives with more traditional moral convictions, took offence. Conservative MP for Luton South, Graham Bright, sponsored a private members bill which would increase the penalties for private entertainment for financial gain without a licence. Fines up to £20,000 or a gaol sentence up to 6 months or both were proposed for holding an unlicensed private entertainment. The effect of this measure has been to criminalise a whole section of the youth population as the hedonistic search for the 'right to party' inevitably continued into the illegal sector. As Steve Redhead argued at the time, the previous legislation was very piecemeal and little known. For instance, the obscure Private Places of Entertainments Act is the relevant by-law, which many local authorities had in fact not adopted before the "media hype about acid house/rave culture".(11) Graham Bright argued that the parties disturb the peace of other people, encourage "drug distribution, fraud and extortion" and are a safety hazard (meaning both in terms of fire on the premises or drivers in a drug induced state filling up the roads at night time).(12)

The 'financial killings', reputedly made by the organisers were, according to Hely and Collin, few and far between.(13) Joy lost thousands of pounds at the rave in August 1989, since they had counted on at least 6,000 people when they set up their equipment comprising of a massive P.A. system, tents, fair attractions, lasers and projection equipment days in advance. In the event only 2,000 turned up. A big profit could have been made if everything had gone right, but the risks are great. The organisers of Energy claim that: "The one time we were raided, it wiped out all our previous profits".(14) Many of the smaller organisations which had their equipment confiscated were bankrupted in the process. In the end only big 'Firm' backed parties were possible in order to survive the risk of police interference and the legal fees. Bigger party organisations, such as Joy, Live the Dream and Sunrise, employed legal advice on the premises in order to solve any problems with the police. Smaller ones were simply prevented from letting an event occur. This type of professionalism took away some of the sense of adventure for the punters. Ticket prices inflated accordingly, from around £5 in 1988 to £20 for a mega-party in 1989. The gangster element was not attractive either: many ravers found it not very enticing to be in a friendly mood whilst being surrounded by a 'gorilla' security force armed with baseball bats and Doberman dogs.(15)

The winter of 1989-90 saw a few parties hidden in far away locations where a small police force was unable to undertake any action. For example Blackburn had only six P.C.s on duty on a Saturday night, which on one weekend resulted in a party held next door to the police station. By spring 1990, the then Greater

Manchester Police Chief Constable James Anderton stepped in, and with the help of Lancashire police, many raids were executed, successfully preventing any more pay parties from occurring in Blackburn. Parties were forced into more and more obscure places, like the previously unexplored orbit of Leeds or 'hidden' in Shropshire.

Rave culture did continue, but it was mostly forced back in the clubs again. However, the police had gained new powers. From 1990, licences could be reviewed seven times a year, instead of - as previously - once a year. In Manchester, clubs like Konspiracy and The Haçienda had to defend their licences in court. The former club lost its battle, but in July 1990, The Haçienda was allowed an extra 6 months with its case being adjourned. Eventually, in 1991, it was granted the right to retain its licence. However, in 1990, the price to pay was to keep out the very 'Acid Ted' that had contributed to the club's popularity. Even *The Sun* realised that some of the sting had been taken out of 'that' Acid House thing when, on July 26, it allowed the following editorial by R. Littlejohn: "The police are out of control. Most of these kids are just out to have a good time". As pop-writer Sarah Champion pointed out, the article then continued in favour of The Haçienda and 'warehouses'.(16)

At the end of 1990, the 'Acid Ted' could be found in little clubs in low profile places like Delight in Shelly's Lazerdome in Stoke-on-Trent. It drew people from as far away as Leeds, Liverpool, Manchester, Birmingham or even Buxton. After close-down at 2.30 a.m. 'Rave Slaves' would congregate at Knutsford Service Station (like many other Service Stations along motorways, such as the M6 or the M62) in order to recover, to stretch out the night a bit and to receive a free fanzine. In good entrepreneurial spirit, the fanzine, *Outa Control*, was financially supported by the organiser of the club night in Stoke, so that its readership felt compelled to come back to his club. At the same time a sense of belonging, created by an attitude of being pitted against police surveillance, was established. Some of the motorway service stations eventually reacted by closing down early in order "to keep the Acid House from coming in".(17) Delight stopped in 1991 and like many provincial clubs, Shelly's Lazerdome has now disappeared into obscurity. Other places such as Coventry's Eclipse have held out longer. Small places still host big club events, such as Renaissance which is open from Saturday night until Sunday morning.

A new feature since 1991 were 'Gay Raves' in the North West, events in rather large clubs, which occur once a month and for which transport is provided: coaches from Liverpool, Nottingham, Leeds, Sheffield and Manchester ensure that all these places are visited on a regular schedule.

From the 'moral panic' of the tabloid press to the introduction of the 'Bright Bill', there runs a discourse of the suppression of the Other, defined as "youth-as-trouble, youth-in-trouble" and as a forbidden hedonistic "youth-as-fun".(18) The law-abiding citizen figure had been offended. According to Dick Hebdige, a subculture is formed "in the space between surveillance and the evasion of surveillance".(19) This means that (young) people display their difference to the establishment which has the power to police certain patterns of consumption. The next section will discuss whether the rave-cult presents some kind of resistance as a spectacular ritual, thereby posing a threat to the subordinating symbolic order.(20)

Sources

1.   E. W. Said, *Orientalism*, (1985), Peregrine Books, p.94.

2.   H. Foster, 'Readings in Cultural Resistance', in *Recodings: Art, Spectacle, Cultural Politics*, (1985), Bay Press.

3.   S. Redhead and A. Melechi, 'The Fall of the Acid Reign', in *New Statesman and Society*, 23/30 December, 1988.

4.   *The Sun*, November 24, 1988.

5.   *The Sun*, November 7, 1988.

6.   *Manchester Evening News*, March 4, 1989.

7.   *The Sun*, June 26, 1989.

8.   *Manchester Evening News*, July, 1989.

9.   Mark Heley and Matthew Collin, 'Summer of Love 1989', in *i-D*, September 1989.

10. Tony Colston-Hayter, 'Why should having fun be against the law?' *The Independent,* March 3, 1990.

11. Steve Redhead, 'Rave Off: Youth, Subculture and the Law', in *Social Science Review,* Vol. 6, No. 3, 1991.

12. Graham Bright, 'Why should having fun be against the law?' *The Independent,* March 3, 1990.

13. M. Heley and M. Collin, op cit.

14. M. Heley and M. Collin, op cit.

15. Although Tony Colston-Hayter, from the Sunrise Organisation, maintained "We are not shadowy gangsters but entrepreneurs meeting a demand for an alternative to glitzy, pretentious night clubs". *The Independent,* March 3, 1990.

16. Sarah Champion, *And God Created Manchester,* (1990) Wordsmith, Manchester. p.119.

17. Knutsford Service Station security man, April 1991.

18 Dick Hebdige, *Hiding in the Light,* Comedia, p.27.

19. Ibid, p.35.

20. Ibid, p.18.

Eternal

> The cycle leading from opposition to defusion, from resistance
> to incorporation encloses each successive subculture.
> Dick Hebdige (1979).(1)

A 'spectacular subculture' is noticed by the public eye because it
breaks with established codes. It is usually originated and
maintained by 'young' people. Youth is not only a social category, a
group that has simply been named because it has a certain age: it is a
psychological category of people who are at a moment of change; a
gap exists between two discourses, that of irresponsible subservient
childhood and of initiative-taking adulthood. At such a moment of
'passage', unconventional ideas may be 'foregrounded', confusing
established categories and offending the symbolic order (in this essay,
by the symbolic order it is meant the ideological position in which the
subject has been placed through culturally determined symbolic
communication, such as language). Gramsci uses the term
'hegemony' to explain that the ruling classes stay in position because
of the acceptance of the status quo in the form of 'common sense' by
"those in practice subordinated to it".(2) This 'common sense'
concerns morality and aesthetics. The expression of transgression,
the challenge to hegemony, is expected to be made apparent through
style, or "rituals of consumption".(3) Thus, young people 'pose' in
order to "pose a threat", to "challenge the symbolic order which
guarantees their subordination".(4)

In the late 80s the (stereotypical) dress sense of the original raver,
both male and female, was baggy, over sized T-shirts, baggy shorts,
track suit bottoms, baggy jeans, even baggy (shapeless) haircuts.
Apart from being comfortable, the clothes were brightly coloured and
relatively cheap. It could even be said that initially there was no
'style' at all, in the sense that no-one really cared about how they
looked; it just had to feel good. Since the 80s could be seen as the
Designer Decade, this type of attitude was a significant departure
from, or a resistance to, the established trend of packaging. It
contrasted with the image produced by the Paris-dominated fashion
world, where women were presented as 'real' (i.e. 'post-feminist')
women, with tight dresses that were cut in at the waist and high
heels, and where the men were wearing suits. The shapeless hair
was also a spit in the eye of the 'sculptured' haircuts that major

hairdressing salons, such as Vidal Sassoon's, created. The usual club goer dresses up to go out dancing. The raver, however, dressed down. This could be called an anti-fashion statement: no-one wanted to be (seen as) a 'fashion victim'. Using semiotics, one may compare an anti-style to an anti-language which, according to Hodge and Kress, "marks on oppositional and marginalised group", whilst "a 'high' culture and language normally signify the values of the dominant group"(5) It can therefore be assumed that the 'lack' of style is a style in itself which marks the identity and difference as a 'marginalised' social group. People who did not belong to 'the scene' were immediately recognised by the fact that they wore tight uncomfortable clothing, like dresses and make-up or a shirt and tie. In this context *The Sunday Times* stated in October 1988: "The hordes that came were not the regular designer-label disco-music devotees, but a hotchpotch of traditionally marginalised adolescents...."(6)

Perhaps these events could be interpreted as a premeditated gesture of resistance by a traditionally marginalised category, defined as 'working class youth'. However, it is more likely that the dress sense of the raver was not a style of conscious choice that posed and possessed a threat. Pierre Bourdieu points out that the consumption of 'high' art displays 'ease', which is a freedom allowed by a surplus of money.(7) The consumption of designer goods shows a similar kind of 'ease'. If there is a threat to be found in these clothes (and if it is indeed a working class style) then it is in the first instance the threat of 'vulgarity', which is the test of necessity. A rave DJ who started out at warehouse parties and who played at several rave related clubs, like the Thunderdome in Manchester, says he had to dress down in order to be accepted by the punters: "the kids that went to the Thunderdome came from sort of council estates and they could only afford certain clothes...."(8)

Not only the lack of finance, but also the intensive dancing and the use of the drug Ecstasy(9) determined the style. It makes a person sweat, so baggy cotton clothing is the most comfortable to wear. Make up is useless in those circumstances, because it would simply 'wash' off in a short time. The euphoria caused by the excitement of the rave events, the excessive body movement and drug use all interfere with a person's sense of balance: high heels are therefore definitely 'out of order' from a raver's point of view. Firm comfortable shoes, preferably with bouncy soles made more sense, hence the emergence of baseball shoes, trainers, Timberlands and

Kickers. The use of 'E' (in contrast to abuse of the same drug) breaks down mental defence mechanisms and "opens the heart" (10); it means that relaxed attitudes are 'in' and therefore restrictive clothing is definitely 'out'. The result was that the wearer looked like an overgrown toddler, which seems to indicate a complete refusal to grow up, to fit into the official 'rational' restrictive world. As the style entered the consumption race, labels like Naf Naf, Mau Mau and the children's clothing manufacturer Chipie became popular. For a short while Kickers were worn which were pretty 'naff' too, i.e. 'unfashionable' and childish. 'E' makes the skin sensitive to textures, which is why women sometimes indulged in silk, purely for the pleasure it gave to themselves. In Freudian terms, 'E' made the user return to a pre-Oedipal stage, where libidinous pleasure is not centred in the genitals, but where sexuality is polymorphous and where sensuality engages the entire body.(11) (Considering that the rave scene developed during the advance of AIDS, which makes penetrative sex a fatal possibility, this was not, socially, a bad thing).

The baggy, comfort conscious dress sense, then, became a style in its own right. Other details were added, like skull caps and 'ethnic' prints, which were part of the revival of psychedelic imagery. Many enthusiastic journalists and other cultural producers nostalgically traced back the stolen signifiers of the first 'Summer of Love' in 1967 (which was a mythical event in itself) and the hippie counter culture that was associated with it. The use of mind altering drugs, strobes, liquid slides, bandanas, the talk of 'love', the appearance of 'day-glo' coloured clothes, the idea of a 'trance dance'; it all added up to the conclusion that the 'Summer of Love' had returned in 1988, this time in Britain. People started to look for ways to make a "pastiche" of hippiedom. (12) For instance Genesis P. Orridge, of the occult band Psychic T.V., suddenly found his niche in 1988 when he heard of the music term 'Acid House', thinking that like Acid Rock in the 1960s it had something to do with hippy-psychedelia. Without hearing it, he dug out his old record collection and started to make new versions of Beach Boys-type tunes.(13) Even so, Acid House has a rather schizophrenic and psychedelic 'feel' not unlike Acid Rock. The texture of the bass-line continually changes and voices and other fragments of stolen sounds make a 'disembodied' appearance. The 'Acid' (the wobbly random synth sequence, originally produced by a Roland TR303 which had lost its programmes) is secured by a 'frame' of an instant four quarter beat at around 125 beats per minute (14), which in effect enhances its hypnotic appeal.

Now the 'look', the appearance, of the psychedelic sixties was sampled. An example of using the hippy cult as a simulacrum, an "identical copy for which no original ever existed"(15), is the following statement by Leo Stanley who owns the Mancunian (rave) clothes shop Identity: "I got the *Woodstock* video out of the video library and checked out what the people were wearing".(16) The result was the return of tie-dye T-shirts, ponchos and other sixties garb, except that the jeans never got tight. The raver started to look like a 'hyperreal'(17) Disneyland hippy, living the dream of hope and happiness (the term 'Disneyland' is useful, because in Disneyland the Mickey Mouse doll does not represent a real mouse, but the cartoon image of one); its connotations with the counter-culture of the 1960s frightened the moral establishment more than one might have expected. Other people, most likely already 'drop outs', were genuinely inspired by the old counter-cultural ideals. As a result, they set up alternative forms of production and consumption, such as the magazine *Encyclopaedia Psychedelia International* in 1988-89. This had, apart from music reviews, bits of yippy philosophy and a psychedelic style of graphic design with optical illusions and collage images using flowers and cut-out grins, that influenced other designers, like those of *i-D* magazine. Others started up 'anarchist' House Systems, sound systems that set up free open-air raves.(18) It can therefore be argued that it does not really matter how or why the style of the raver came about: with its 'statement' of anti-consumerism, pro-vulgarity, anti-rationalism, anti-phallocentrism, the return of the 'hippy' and being young as an attitude, the rave-cult emitted a definite counter-cultural 'air' or appearance.

The details were stylised and the 'look' became a marketable product in a society where the fashion industry has to keep up with latest trends that are associated with youth or eternal rejuvenation. As Hebdige puts it, "stripped of its unwholesome connotations, the style becomes fit for public consumption".(19) By the summer of 1989, department stores like C&A were stocked up with lilac and orange T-shirts: even a child could wear the 'colourful garb'. The Parisian fashion house Chanel, "that bastion of classicism", brought out a money pouch or 'bum bag'(20), which is a small bag that straps around the waist, leaving body movement unrestricted and preventing belongings from getting lost in the middle of the frenzy. Ravers were caught in a maze of consumerism in order to stay ahead of recuperation, in the process eating up signs of other subcultures, thereby incorporating and attracting a wide and plural cross section of British youth. Items like hip-hop style leather baseball shoes, football fan casual style, Salford 'scally' flared and baggy trousers, or hippy style floppy velvet hats were all spotted at raves or rave-related events at some time or another. Short sleeved T-shirts gave way to long sleeved ones and then the 'holy' hooded top was added. The latter was again a matter of practicality; when a party is over, the feeling of fatigue and the effect of cooling down requires something warm that can wrap the entire body. The details on baseball shoes could change monthly but in the end they were replaced by Kickers and the already established Timberlands (at least in the North West of England).

The elitist 'subcultural' style magazines *The Face* and *i-D* announced that, in 1990, Londoners dug up long-deleted 'old school' trainers in the hope that no-one could get hold of these in any mass amounts, thereby contradicting the concept of 'vulgarity', which was merely present as an appearance. As with avant-garde art, a creative expression in style is devalued either because it is simply popular, or because it has lost its exclusive meaning.[21] Only an elite, who often claimed to be the 'originals', were able to keep up with the financial demands of this mad consumption race. These were mostly people in their mid- to late-twenties, with reasonably well paid jobs in the fashion, communications or (entrepreneurial) entertainment sectors. With an amazing speed chain-stores adapted themselves to fast changes in detail. If these refinements in detail were not noticed, it seemed like this was not a subculture at all; its signifiers were openly available to the public eye. But its meanings (i.e. the hedonistic pursuit of all things pleasurable and reaching a total state of void through intoxication by music, dance and drugs) were reduced to nothing, making them a pure appearance (yet another simulacrum) in the process. By 1989, real toddlers were spotted in raver's outfits.

By 1992, the hooded top had vanished completely. Baggy clothes are still the most practical, although most of what can be seen to be worn are either faded and so, perhaps, old. After the popularity of all-white gear in 1990 during a period where Ambient House seemed to be popular, there were lycra body suits, inspired by the singer of Deee-lite, for women. See-through blouses can be seen in the club environment, while cycling face-masks in Altern-8 fashion can be spotted at events which may be interpreted as contemporary raves.

One of the reasons why high street stores were able to keep up and become part of the mass appeal of the rave-event, was because of new companies like Joe Bloggs from Manchester and Funky Junky. The trade name of Joe Bloggs signifies 'the-man-in-the-street', but the sale techniques are sophisticated. At the same time as catering for 'hard core' shops, it sold its products to high street shops such as Top Man.(22) Free clothes were provided to prominent key figures in the rave-cult, such as the Happy Mondays, in order to gain street credibility. Shaun Ryder, lead-singer in the band, would not have minded: "We are Thatcher's children" is one of his famous truisms, a statement which interferes with a prevailing counter-cultural critical logic. Funky Junky employs "a team of workers (all under 18) who regularly comb the clubs and raves in search of new ideas", which he sells off to department stores like Debenhams. The teenage owner of the company was quoted as saying that "Tony Colston-Hayter (the man behind the massive Sunrise raves) has captured the mass market".(23)

Just to illustrate the completion of the process of recuperation, NatWest Bank brought out a student magazine,*The Edge,* which in 1990 published an article on clubs in Brighton, where people "go mental" (which means that they are or act like, ravers).(24) It makes one wonder if a threat was ever present. For most of its life span in 1988-90, the rave-cult was not, as is conventionally thought, a subculture, but rather a form of popular culture that mesmerised, at the same time, style-elitists, 'drop-outs' and a great section of working class youth, as well as the English criminal justice system. As Fredric Jameson put it:

> ...local counter-cultural forms of cultural resistance...are all somehow secretly disarmed and absorbed by a system of which they themselves might well be considered a part, since they can achieve no distance from it.(25)

To try and find a depth beneath the aesthetic of the rave-event is like trying to deflate a bouncy castle (a favourite feature at open air raves): all that can be found is air and an affirmation of a Thatcherite enterprise culture, leaving its shape, the representation of the dream of 'love', hope and happiness, deflated in the process. This would be a sad conclusion, which does little justice to the feeling of elation that a rave event could give to its participants. Neither does it explain the moral panic of the 'righteous' citizen, whose view on the world is shaped by representations that reconfirm the solidity, the unalterability, of the dominant, or established, symbolic order.

According to Steve Redhead, it is subcultural theories that produce 'authentic' subcultures in the first place, not the other way around. (26) It was only after the stereotype 'Acid Ted' had been established and the rave scene had been criminalised, that an 'underground' form of mass entertainment could be identified, a youth culture which is both very young in age and provincial in background.

Perhaps it will be helpful to look at some of the immediate historical sources of the formalist aspects of the rave in order to give it a place on the cultural map. Rather than creating a spectacle of resistance or 'alternative' patterns of living, the rave offered a release from day to day realities, a temporary escapist disappearance like the weekend or holiday. It was never felt that a critical distance was necessary. Rather, there was an offensive against the established order by negating its rationale, through the surrender to a void. A Dionysian (27) ritual of dance and hedonism evolved, whereby the established 'self' was undone.

Sources

1. Dick Hebdige, *Subculture: The Meaning of Style*, (1979), Methuen, p.100.

2. Raymond Williams, *Keywords*, (1983), Fontana, p.145.

3. Dick Hebdige, op cit, p.103.

4. Dick Hebdige, *Hiding in the Light*, (1988), Comedia, p.18.

5. R. Hodge & G. Kress, *Social Semiotics*, (1988), Polity Press, p.87.

6. Max Prangnell, 'The Summer of Acid House Hype', *The Sunday Times*, October 30, 1988.

7. Pierre Bourdieu, 'The Aristocracy of Culture', in *Media,*

Culture and Society, (1980) Vol. 2.

8.   Steve Williams, personal interview, December 12, 1991.

9.   The amphetamine MDMA or 'E', a dance drug (see introduction).

10.   Jay Stevens, *Storming Heaven, LSD and the American Dream,* (1989) Paladin, p.487.

11.   Sigmund Freud, 'Three Essays on the Theory of Sexuality', (1905) in *On Sexuality,* (1977), Penguin, p.100.

12.   Fredric Jameson, 'Postmodernism, or the Cultural Logic of Late Capitalism',*New Left Review,* No. 146.

13.   Stuart Cosgrove, 'Forbidden Fruits', *New Statesman and Society,* September 2, 1988.

14.   Many peoples around the world dance themselves into a kind of state of hypnosis at that particular speed, since it is related to the heart beat in exercise.

15.   Frederic Jameson, op cit.

16.   Jennifer Foote, 'Madchester!', *Newsweek,* July 23, 1990.

17.   Umberto Eco, *Travels in Hypperreality,* (1967) , Picador, (1987), pp.43-48.

18.   Matthew Collin, 'Party On', *i-D,* No. 89, February 1991.

19.   Dick Hebdige, *Subculture: The Meaning of Style,* Ibid, p.130.

20.   Lindsay Baker, 'The Cutting Edge', *The Face,* No. 18, March 1990.

21.   Pierre Bourdieu, op cit.

22.   Lindsay Baker, 'The Cutting Edge', op cit.

23. Ibid.

24. Chris King, 'Brighton Rock', *The Edge*, NatWest, Summer 1990.

25. Fredric Jameson, op cit.

26. Steve Redhead, *The End-of-the-Century Party*, (1990), Manchester University Press, Manchester, p.25.

27. Friedrich Nietzsche, *The Birth of Tragedy*, (1871), Anchor (1956), p.22.

Escape

All you bastards, come here by my side;
don't be so fucking serious!
Seduction (1988).(1)

Dionysian man...realise(s) that no act of (his) can work any
change in the eternal condition of things...
The truth once seen, man is aware of the ghastly absurdity of
existence; nausea invades him...
...art, that sorceress expert in healing, approaches him; only
she can turn his fits of nausea into the imaginations with which
it is possible to live. The sublime subjugates terror in art while
the comic spirit releases us through art from the tedium of
absurdity.
Friedrich Nietzsche (1870-1).(2)

In his orgiastic hour of worship, he annihilates himself and his
terror...
Monroe C. Beardsley (1966).(3)

If youth style magazines such as *i-D* and *The Face* can be believed,
the rave scene historically started in Ibiza. This is the place where
bohemians used to hang out and where the hippie-trail ended on its
return journey. Then it became a target for package tours and 18-30
Club holidays, making it "the toilet of the Englishman abroad".(4)
This type of tourist was based in San Antonio. On the other side of
the island was Ibiza Town, where the rich, the fashion conscious and
the sexually transgressive entertained themselves in clubs like
Amnesia or Manhattans. A small group of mainly London tourists
escaped the thug-mentality and the crying-kids-with-ice-creams
syndrome and surrendered themselves to the delights of Ecstasy and
exoticism in the different clubs of Ibiza Town from midnight till well
into the following day. Appearing again into the daylight somewhere
in the afternoon, frightened families would horde their children
away from these tired and degenerate looking beings.(5)   The
atmosphere was unlike anything in Britain, it was purely hedonistic
and rather in 'bad' taste; the music was a (Balearic) mixture of
anything remotely danceable. However, it was felt that "if you take
mind blowing drugs at the same time, you will want to recreate this

event".(6)

In the autumn of 1987, Ibiza veteran DJ Paul Oakenfold smuggled his friends into his "Project Club in Streatham after it had closed at 2 a.m." to relive a little "bit of Ibiza".(7) At that time British club life was in need of a new idea or concept, so this ready-made event was an excellent opportunity to put some fresh energy into night life. In November of that year, Jenny and Danny Rampling opened the Shoom Club, using the hippy and holiday Smiley logo as an identity tag. It was a more or less overnight success; within weeks people needed to be turned away from its doors. Inside everybody danced, whether they wanted to or not. Since it was frequented by people with a 'hippy mentality', the relatively small room was pumped full of smoke which, together with continuous strobe-lights, exaggerated the effect of disorientation. The punters wore clothes which were of that unselfconscious quality "that only tends to afflict British people when abroad".(8) Gradually House music was adopted as a form of identity. This then was replaced by a new musical form called Acid House, with all the 'unsavoury' connotations of its name and the intrinsic ability to help the listener to lose herself completely in its hypnotic sound.

> 'Shooming' is the state of ecstasy dancers aspire to, losing themselves in Bam Bam's rhythms in order to leave the real world behind.(9)

Other clubs such as Spectrum and The Trip took over the concept. At the peak of its development, in May 1988, one-off parties like the three Hedonism-events were organised.

According to one participant, these parties attracted a real mixture of people; fashion victims, 'gays' and working class people "who had caught on to it quickly".(10) It is important to notice, that the actual initiators were "all in their late twenties".(11) They were people who had been living on the cutting edge, the space where new ideas evolve and who were mainly connected with the fashion or music industry. They were part of 'marginalised' social groups such as the gay community and the bohemian subculture of (illegal) drug users. It may be possible to compare this group of people with the 'hipster' as described by Norman Mailer. The 'hipster' is part of an elite, with "a language most adolescents can understand instinctively, for the hipster's intense view of existence matches their experience...."(12)

In Manchester a similar escalation of events occurred, except that there the music had arrived first. From 1986 onwards, Stu Allen introduced House music to a Mancunian audience on local Piccadilly Radio. Around the same time, Martin Prendergast and Mike Pickering played House Music in the Haçienda club on the traditional 'lads-night-out', the Friday night. Gradually its audience shifted from being mainly black to predominantly white and male.

Around January 1988 the drug Ecstasy appeared on the Manchester club scene. That summer the London inspired HOT-night started in the Haçienda on Wednesday nights, which was a 'total holiday experience' including the addition of a little swimming pool. People turned up in beach wear, enjoyed the free ice lolly pops, became in a sense more androgynous and felt mellow in a smoke filled space enveloped by a 'Balearic' mix of garage music, hybrids of House music and sampled 'breaks' like those of streaming water.

That summer Martin Prendergast left and was replaced by Graeme Park. The Friday night became an event where it felt as though a goal was scored for as long as the night permitted. There was a chaotic noise of Acid House and Techno drumbeats, whistles and ecstatic shouts. Egos melted in the sweltering frenzied heat of the mass of sweating bodies.

Language, that Apollonian creator of the symbolic order, was unable to catch the event; participants of any rave event do not seem to be able to describe their experience as anything else than, "it was wild", "absolutely unbelievable, there wasn't anything like it", "great", "mental" or "this is not dancing, this is a religion". The master(ing) gaze had disappeared. For this reason, dancing to show off had gone, even though a communal adoration occurred because people piled onto the stage or anything else that was raised above the crowd. In order to get 'higher, higher'. This was the dance in which to forget, to loose oneself; this was the Dionysian ritual of obliteration, of disappearance.

If we note the glorious transport which arises in man at the shattering of the principium individuationis, then we are in a position to apprehend the essence of Dyonysiac rapture, whose closest analogy is furnished by physical intoxication, through narcotic potions or the approach of spring.(13)

The consumption pattern of high entry fees and expensive drugs (the price of 'E' escalated according to its popularity up to around £20) resulted in a complete disappearance of the value of money. There was an immediate urge to buy the clothes that others wore, a 'sheep mentality' which resulted in certain colours such as lilac gaining overnight popularity. Expensive beach clothes such as 100% Mambo and Body Glove became prevalent and there was a proliferation of 'top-of-the-range' footwear, with trainers costing up to £100. The free market dream of Margaret Thatcher and the New Right, the unrestrained mode of consumption supported by credit cards and an entrepreneurial spirit, was taken to its ultimate limit. This went beyond the conservative moral 'common sense' that is supposed to keep the work-force in its place.

As police surveillance intensified, parties were held at increasingly obscure places, ravers would drive into the night, at times in convoys, music blasting and spirits high on energetic 'vibes'. Sometimes the destination would never be found, giving the ambiguous pleasure of being part of a conspiracy and a sense of adventure of travelling into the unknown. Besides, anything seemed better than being back home in the mundane environment of daily reality. The long night suspends a feeling of an everlasting present.

> Night is a special time....They are times when social syntagms lose their force....The availability of these oppositional practices is mapped on to social time and space, organised into a system of domains.(14)

Like holidays, nightlife is a moment in which the established order is undone, where one can relax. It does not seek to criticise it but rather to escape it. In this way, a 'double-language situation' occurs, the formal and the informal, the public and the private self. Mikhail Bakhtin once pointed out that popular culture, as opposed to 'serious culture', is a model of life that has been repressed with the rise of class society. He labels it as being a Carnival, the culture of laughter and reversal and of cyclical time, where like in the season of spring, death and rebirth are confused. Spring can give a feeling of hope, a sense of future, which was expressed in the names of rave-events such as Sunrise and Future.

The essence of carnival lies in change, in death-rebirth, in destructive-creative time; carnivalistic images are basically ambivalent.(15)

It escapes the theoretical ideal that official culture can provide, the forcing of identities that recuperates all cultural and creative production.

Jean Baudrillard points out that the avant-garde within the framework of (official) art attempts to escape recuperation, by defying the "seduction of the gaze", so that "modern art exerts only the magic of disappearance".(16) Within popular culture the attempt to evade surveillance can be of vital importance. Its official framework is that of criminal law, which became increasingly oppressive as the New 'Moral Right' government in Britain in the 1980s invaded private space, with the Local Act, 1988, section 28, clause 25 of the Criminal Justice Bill, anti-abortion Bills, the Video Recordings Act, 1984 - a law against 'video nasties' - or trials set up in order to prosecute adults having SM sex. Night life is restrained by licensing laws which force clubs to close at 2 a.m. and which now, under the Licensing Act, 1988, enable the police to review a club licence several times a year. This process of invasion, initiated by the press, can create a moral panic which might result in an increased interference with freedom of movement and expression. In the end, disappearance is the only 'tactic' left to find a release, an escape, a moment of moving to the other side of the mirror which is held up by established discourses such as the media discourse, as a 'fixed' identity.

It could be argued that the use of a dance-drug like 'Ecstasy' in a rave environment makes one 'return' to a stage in psychological development which is before the acquisition of language, thereby undoing the self that is constituted in and by language and in and by its constructed discourse. A break is caused with the established symbolic order at a basic level, however temporary. This could possess a greater threat than simply to pose a subcultural style within the context of a so-called 'dominant culture'. A 'subcultural style' would simply affirm the established order of society by being 'different' from (and therefore defined by) this order. In this case there was a surrender to a complete void of meaning, rather than some form of resistance.

Beyond the binary oppositions of private-public self or death-rebirth, it is difficult to find an opposition with regards to politics. By dissolving the self, no counter-culture was established which offered an alternative. When one is in opposition, the thing that is opposed is acknowledge. When one escapes instead of opposes, no alternative moral values are proposed at all. This lack of dialectic is what Baudrillard would call 'amoral', rather than immoral.(17) Like an amorphous monster, the 'amoral' raver went 'mental', creating at times a sense of profound panic in the people who desired to make sense of it all. This may add to the explanation of the moral panic that took hold of the 'establishment', which (in different guises) attempted to give the rave-cult a (negative) place within the relative safety of a dialectic representation. Since 'unregulated' rave-events could involve thousands of people, it may be understandable that to some people their weekend or night out appeared indeed as a "Wild Revolution".(18)

Sources

1.   Seduction, *Seduction*, Break Out, A & M Records, 1988.

2.   Friedrich Nietzsche, *The Birth of Tragedy*, (1956), Anchor, p.51.

3.   M. C. Beardsley, *Aesthetics from Classical Greece to the Present*, (1966) University of Alabama Press, p.276.

4.   John Godfrey, 'Happy Daze Are Here Again', *i-D*, No. 59, June 1988.

5.   Andy, personal interview, February 1991.

6.   Paul Cons, personal interview, February 1991.

7.   John Godfrey, op cit.

8.   David Roberts, 'The Grin Factor', *Sky Magazine*, October 1988.

9.   John Godfrey, op cit.

10.   Paul Cons, op cit.

11. Paul Cons, op cit.

12. Norman Mailer, 'The White Negro', *Advertisements for Myself*, (1959), Andre Deutsch, p.288.

13. Friedrich Nietzsche, op cit, p.22.

14. R. Hodge & G. Kress, *Social Semiotics*, (1988) Polity Press, pp.66-68.

15. Mikhail Bakhtin, quoted in Tzvetan Todorov, *Mikhail Bakhtin: the Dialogical Principle*, (1984), Manchester University Press.

16. Jean Baudrillard, *The Ecstasy of Communication*, (1988), Semiotext(e), p.34.

17. Ibid, p.81.

18. As seen on a skateboarder cum ravers T-shirt.

Chill out

> The world we know is not this ultimately simple configuration where events are reduced to accentuate their essential traits, their final meaning, or their initial and final value. On the contrary, it is a profusion of entangled events. Michel Foucault.(1)

In analysing the event of the rave, different representations have appeared. Depending on the context and the discourses employed which asked "what is it?", a different answer could be posited; the 'establishment' installed a 'scapegoat' in order to define the social norms(2), art historians found a (sub)cultural event(3), some observers noticed a 'disappearance'(4) and participants indulged in a 'dream' of hope and happiness.(5)

As the 'moral panic' developed, a conflict between the idea of free enterprise and a conservative hierarchical social structure became apparent. Law-abiding citizens(6) were positioned in contrast to fantasies of an evil cult that congregates at mass sex-and-drug orgies.(7) At first, the police were not very interested in a relatively small number of people engaging in the intake of illegal substances such as Ecstasy, even though it was listed as a Class A drug under the Misuse of Drugs Act 1971. It was only when thousands of people became involved, attending large social gatherings after the entertainment curfew of 2 a.m. and seen to be enjoying themselves like the 'rich', that the social order was 'destabilised'.

A fast working communication network resulted in an acceleration of events. Publicity resulted in the increase of business for rave organisers, which in return created more publicity and yet more business for party organisers, record companies, clothes manufacturers (especially for T-shirt printers), drug dealers, newspapers and eventually even academics. As Hal Foster has argued:

> ...difference is often fabricated in the interest of social control as well as of commodity innovation.(8)

An identity was established in the process, which was distilled into the 'Acid Ted' who roamed the motorways on Friday and Saturday nights with fellow teenagers in search of good times. Alternatively, ravers can be found at unlikely locations around Europe(9), in Los Angeles(10), or even on the coast of Thailand.(11)

Cultural analysts attempted to place the rave-cult within the eternal conceptual cycle of resistance and recuperation. Yet, Western society operates within a virtually inescapable electronic network; it is therefore difficult to imagine a "critical distance".(12)   In the participation of raves, no other motivation could be found than that of escape from daily realities.   This is a kind of conceptual disappearance of the constituted self. A physical disappearance occurred as well; once police started to harass parties and 'associated' clubs, raves began to occur outside the limelight of city centres.

When Graham Bright supported the proposal for increased penalties for unregulated private entertainment (i.e. without a licence) there was only one overt sign of resistance: the 'right to party' movement which staged several demonstrations. This was organised by the overtly entrepreneurial side of rave production. The entrepreneur, Tony Colston-Hayter of Sunrise, appeared on the television chat show of Jonathan Ross, where he poured water over the presenter in a parody of the punk era of the 1970s (appropriately this was in the presence of one time punk music journalist Paul Morley, who seemed to disapprove of everything Tony Colston-Hayter represented). Tony Colston-Hayter put forward the case of free enterprise and the freedom to have fun, which surfaced most clearly in his polemic with Graham Bright published in *The Independent*(13) newspaper before the 'Bright Bill' on 'Acid House' became law.

Whilst examining these, at times, irreconcilable representations, it is important not to lose sight of the participants' (aesthetic) experience. The presence of the polymorphous raver was as much responsible for the 'magic' of the night as its ideological framework. It was the state of bliss achieved by losing the self in the 'anonymity' of fellow ravers and in 'blinding' music, that made everything worthwhile. The resulting inability to articulate a position created an ambivalence of meaning, so that "even the protagonist of the secret would not know how to betray it".(14)

Sources

1. Michel Foucault, 'Nietzsche, Genealogy, History', in Paul Rainbow (ed.), *The Foucault Reader*, (1986), Peregrine Books, Penguin, p.89.

2. Hal Foster, Readings in Cultural Resistance, *Recodings: Art, Spectacle, Cultural Politics*, (1985), Bay Press, p.166.

3. *Living the Dream* was inspired by the work of subcultural theorist and art historian Dick Hebdige, expressed by *Subculture: The Meaning of Style*, (1979), Methuen.

4. Mostly inspired by the work of Jean Baudrillard, such as 'The Masses', in Mark Poster (ed.), *Jean Baudrillard: Selected Writings*, (1989), Polity Press, pp.213-214.

5. For example: 'Choci, Can You Feel It?', *Road*, Autumn 1990.

6. Graham Bright, 'Why should having fun be against the law?', *The Independent*, March 3, 1990.

7. Tabloid Press, such as *The Sun*, November 7, 1988.

8. Hal Foster, op cit, p.167.

9. Lindsay Baker, (ed.), 'Ravers' Guide to Europe', *The Face*, No. 23, August 1990.

10. Gary, personal interview, September 1990 "...mainly pop stars and people who earned their money out of the rave scene."

11. Lisa, personal interview, February 1991 "...people in their early twenties with jobs like hairdressing. It seemed like they had saved money for a once in a life-time experience, before slotting back into society."

12. Fredric Jameson, 'Postmodernism, or the Cultural Logic of Late Capitalism', *New Left Review*, No. 146.

13. Tony Colston-Hayter, 'Why should having fun be against the law'?, *The Independent*, March 3, 1990.

14. Jean Baudrillard, *The Ecstasy of Communication*, (1988), Semiotext(e), p.65.

Bibliography

Books

Aggleton, Peter, *Deviance*, (1987), Tavistock.

Barthes, Roland, *Mythologies*, translated by Annette Lavers, (1989), Paladin.

Barthes, Roland, *The Pleasure of the Text*, translated by Richard Miller, (1990), Basil Blackwell.

Baudrillard, Jean, *The Ecstasy of Communication*, translated by Bernard and Caroline Schutze, (1988), Semiotext(e) Foreign Agents Series.

Beardsley, Monroe C., *Aesthetics from Classical Greece to the Present, A Short History*, (1966), The University of Alabama Press.

Berger, John, *Ways of Seeing*, (1972), Penguin (1984).

Burgin, Victor, *The End of Art Theory*, (1986), Macmillan.

Chambers, Iain, *Popular Culture: the Metropolitan Experience*, (1986), Methuen.

Champion, Sarah, *And God Created Manchester*, (1990), Wordsmith.

Durant, Alan, *Conditions of Music*, (1984), Macmillan.

Eagleton, Terry, *The Ideology of the Aesthetic*, (1990), Basil Blackwell.

Eco, Umberto, *Travels in Hyperreality*, translated by William Weaver, (1987), Picador Pan.

Foster, Hal, *Recodings; Art, Spectacle, Cultural Politics*, (1985), Bay Press.

Foucault, Michel, *The History of Sexuality*, translated by Robert

Hurley, (1984), Penguin.

Freud, Sigmund, *On Sexuality*, translations by Angela Richards, (1977), Penguin.

Godfrey, John, (ed.), *A decade of i-Deas*, (1990), Penguin.

Hebdige, Dick, *Hiding in the Light*, (1989) Comedia.

Hebdige, Dick, *Subculture: The Meaning of Style*, (1984), Methuen.

Hodge, Robert and Kress, Gunther, *Social Semiotics*, (1988), Polity Press.

Huyssen, Andreas, *After the Great Divide*, (1986), Macmillan.

Kellner, Douglas, *Jean Baudrillard, from Marxism to Postmodernism*, (1986), Black Swan.

Lapsley, Robert and Westlake, Michael, *Film Theory*, (1988), Manchester University Press.

Lucie-Smith, Edward, *Movements in Art since 1945*, (1987), Thames and Hudson.

Mailer, Norman, *Advertisements for Myself*, (1987), Andre Deutsch.

Nietzsche, Friedrich, *The Birth of Tragedy*, translated by Francis Golffing, (1956), Anchor.

Poster, Mark, (ed.), *Jean Baudrillard, selected writings*, (1988), Polity Press.

Rabinow, Paul, (ed.), *The Foucault Reader*, translation by Random House, (1986), Penguin.

Redhead, Steve, *The End-of-the-Century Party*, (1990), Manchester University Press.

Reynolds, Simon, *Blissed Out*, (1990), Serpent's Tail.

Rice, Phillip and Waugh, Patricia,*Modern Literary Theory*, (includes extracts by Saussure, Barthes, Derrida and Kristeva), (1989), Edwards Arnold.

Richter, Hans *Dada Art and Anti-Art*, (1964), translated by David Britt, (1975), Thames and Hudson.

Said, Edward W., *Orientalism*, (1985), Penguin.

Sontag Susan, *A Susan Sontag Reader,* (1982), Penguin.

Stevens, Jay, *Storming Heaven: LSD and the American Dream*, (1984), Penguin.

Todorov, Tzvetan, *Mikhail Bakhtin, the Dialogical Principle*, translated by Wlad Godzich, (1984), Manchester University Press.

Tomlinson, Alan, (ed.), *Consumption, Identity and Style*, (1990), Comedia, Routledge.

Waldberg, Patrick, *Surrealism*, (1978), Thames and Hudson.

Williams, Raymond, *Keywords*, (1989), Black Swan.

Wiseman, Mary Bittner, *The Ecstasies of Roland Barthes*, (1989), Routledge.

Yurick, Sol, *Behold Metatron, the recording angel*, (1985), Semiotext(e) Foreign Foreign Agents Series.

Articles

Baker, Lindsay, 'The Cutting Edge', *The Face,* Vol. 2. No. 18, March 1990.

Baker, Lindsay, (ed.), 'A Raver's Guide to Europe', *The Face,* Vol. 2., No. 23, August 1990.

Beard, Steve, 'Forbidden Fruit', *i-D*, No. 81, June 1990.

Bourdieu, Pierre, 'The Aristocracy of Culture', *Media, Culture and Society,* 1980.

Bright, Graham, 'Why should having fun be against the law?', *The Independent,* March 3, 1990.

'Choci, Can You Feel It?' *Road,* Autumn, 1990.

Collin, Matthew and Heley, Mark, 'Summer of Love 1989', *i-D,* No. 72, September 1989.

Collin, Matthew, 'Singing in the Rain; Manchester', *i-D,* No. 81, June 1990.

Colston-Hayter, Tony, 'Why should having fun be against the law?', *The Independent,* March 3, 1990.

Cosgrove, Stuart, 'Forbidden Fruits', *New Statesman and Society,* September 2, 1988.

Ehrlich, Dimitri, 'Liverpudlian Lightning', *Interview,* August 1990.

Foote, Jennifer, 'Madchester!', *Newsweek,* July 23, 1990.

Garratt, Sheryl, 'Was it London or Manchester Invented Acid House', *The Face,* Vol. 2, No. 18, March 1990.

Godfrey, John, 'Happy Daze Are Here Again', *i-D,* No. 59, June 1988.

Godfrey, John, 'No Sell Out', *i-D,* No. 79, April 1990.

Godfrey, John, 'Hippy Hour', *i-D,* No. 82, July 1990.

Goodwin, Stephen, 'Acid House Bil "aims to target criminal gangs"', *The Times,* March 10, 1990.

Hooton, Peter, 'Footnotes', *The Face,* Vol. 2, No. 26, November 1990.

Jameson, Fredric, 'Postmodernism, or the Cultural Logic of Late Capitalism', *New Left Review,* No. 146.

Jim, Guru, 'House and all that', *Halcyon Daze,* Fac 239, No. 4, 1990.

Joly, Michelle, 'SM - is it a crime?' *i-D,* No. 90, March 1991.

King, Chris, 'Storm Warning & Brighton Rock', *The Edge,* NatWest, September 1990.

King, Martin, 'Smiley's People', *Marxism Today,* October 1988.

Linton, Martin, 'MP wants £20,000 acid house fines', *The Guardian,* March 10, 1990.

Melechi, Antonio, *The Ecstasy of Disappearance,* elsewhere in this collection, originally written Summer 1990 and revised as Chapter 3 of this book.

Melechi, Antonio and Redhead, Steve, 'The Fall of the Acid Reign', *New Statesman and Society,* December 23-30, 1988.

Noon, Mike, 'Freaky', *i-D,* No. 77, February 1990.

Prangnell, Max, 'The Summer of Acid House hype', *The Sunday Times,* October 30, 1988.

Redhead, Steve, 'Rave Off: Youth, Subculture and the Law', *Social Science Review,* Vol. 6, No. 3, 1991.

Rietveld, Hillegonda C. (alias C. Ogden), 'How the young see acid cult parties', *Manchester Evening News,* March 11, 1989.

Rietveld, Hillegonda C. (alias Gonnie), 'Mancunian Candidate', *i-D,* No. 59, June 1988.

Roberts, David, 'The Grin Factor', *Sky Magazine,* October 1988.

Romain, 'C.C.', (ed.), Ecstasy, *Deadline,* No. 12, October 1989.

Ross, Angus, 'Directory', *i-D,* No. 77, February 1990.

Rushton, Neil, 'Out on the Floor', *The Face,* No. 29, September 1982.

Sandall, Robert, 'A music scene to stir the soul', *The Sunday Times,* February 11, 1990.

Sharrock, David, 'Acid House party organisers jailed for breach of injunction', *The Guardian,* November 30, 1989.

Smith, Andrew, 'Raving Mad', *Melody Maker,* July 14, 1990.

Style, James, 'The Acid test for Acid House',*The Independent,* May 23, 1990.

Thornton, Sarah, 'Strategies for Reconstructing the Popular Past', *Popular Music,* Vol. 9/1, 1990.

Toop, David, 'Tripping Quietly', *The Face,* Vol. 2, No. 18, March 1990.

van Veen, Gert, 'Een nieuw komisch orgasme', *De Volkskrant,* December 22, 1990.

Velthoven, Willem, 'Pump up the Picture', *Mediamatic,* Vol. 2, No. 4, June 1988.

Other textual sources (without specific authors)

Daily Mirror, November 14, 1988.

Daily Mirror, January 30, 1990.

Encyclopaedia Psychedelia International, Vol. 11, 1988.

Manchester Evening News, March 4, 1989.

Manchester Evening News, July 17, 1989.

Manchester Evening News, January 30, 1991.

Offbeat, October 1988.

Outa Control, December 1990.

South Manchester Reporter, May 25, 1990.

The Sun , November 7, 1988.

The Sun, November 24, 1988.

The Sun, June 26, 1989.

The Times, March 9, 1990.

Music play-list

The canon of the music played at rave events is enormous and is (to the participants as opposed to DJs) often anonymous, yet its narratives have been a main source of inspiration for the writing of this paper. Research by the same author is now being undertaken into the roots of this canon, House music.

Specifically quoted are:

E-Zee Possee, *Everything Starts with an E,* More Protein, Virgin Records, 1988.

Seduction, *Seduction,* Break Out, A & M Records, 1988.

Anambi, *Burning up Inside,* Rob Records, 1991.

BIG GY

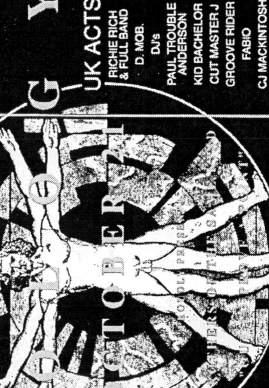

ACTS USA
PUBLIC ENEMY
CONFIRMED

E.P.M.D.
CONFIRMED

BIG DADDY KANE
CONFIRMED

DJ USA
FRANKIE BONE'S

UK ACTS
RICHIE RICH & FULL BAND

D. MOB.

DJ's

PAUL TROUBLE ANDERSON

KID BACHELOR

CUT MASTER J

GROOVE RIDER

FABIO

CJ MACKINTOSH

MORE TO BE CONFIRMED

the edge

FORMERLY THE ECLIPSE

OPEN

1992

COVENTRY

THE EDGE · LOWER FO

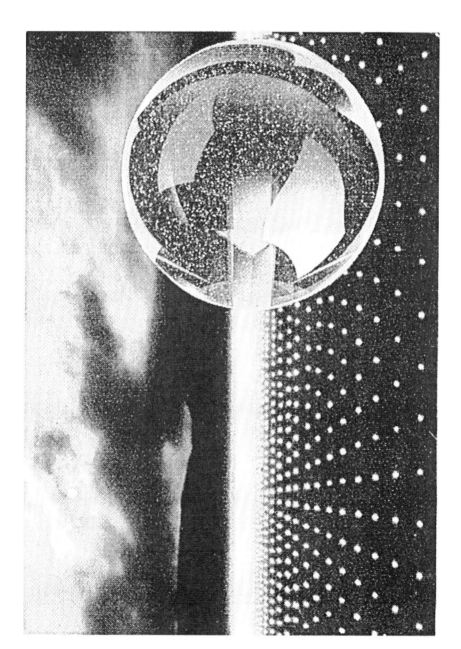

PHANTASY

SATURDAY 30th SEPTEMBER 1989

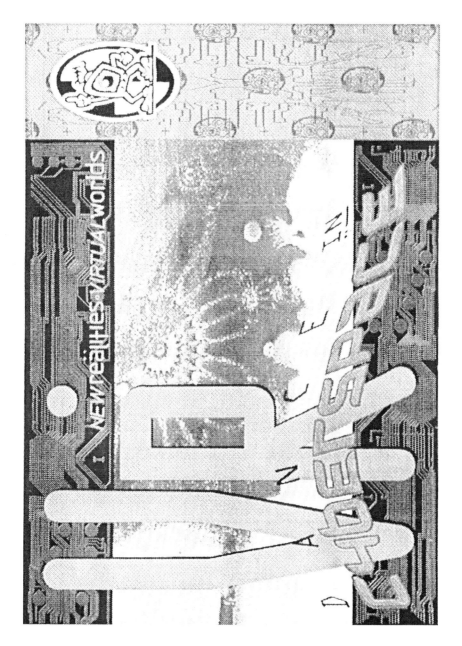

FIVE THIRTY

July Tour

Tuesday	10th	Brighton Zap Club	Tuesday	17th	Leicester Princess Charlotte	Tuesday	24th	Leeds Duchess
Wednesday	11th	Windsor Old Trout	Wednesday	18th	Derby Kid	Wednesday	25th	Doncaster Jug
Thursday	12th	Salisbury Arts Centre	Thursday	19th	Coventry Tic Toc	Thursday	26th	Manchester Boardwalk
Friday	13th	Oxford Jericho Tavern	Friday	20th	Dudley JB's	Friday	27th	Warrington Legends
Saturday	14th	Bath Moles	Saturday	21st	Cambridge Sea Cadet	Sunday	28th	Sheffield Leadmill
Sunday	15th	Bristol Fleece	Monday	23rd	Newcastle Riverside	Sunday	29th	London U.L.U.

AbSTaiN!

FIVE THIRTY

ON TOUR

NOVEMBER MONDAY 5 LIVERPOOL, POLYTECHNIC TUESDAY 6 LEEDS, POLYTECHNIC WEDNESDAY 7 BUCKLEY, TIVOLI THURSDAY 8 LANCASTER, SUGARHOUSE FRIDAY 9 EDINBURGH, THE VENUE SATURDAY 10 GLASGOW, KING TUTS WAH WAH HUT MONDAY 12 NEWCASTLE, RIVERSIDE TUESDAY 13 COVENTRY, SIR TOG WEDNESDAY 14 NOTTINGHAM, TRENT POLYTECHNIC THURSDAY 15 SALISBURY, ARTS CENTRE SATURDAY 17 ALDERSHOT, BUZZ CLUB SUNDAY 18 LONDON, U.L.U. TUESDAY 20 READING, UNIVERSITY WEDNESDAY 21 WINDSOR, OLD TROUT THURSDAY 22 AYLESBURY, CIVIC HALL FRIDAY 23 MARLOW, THE SQUARE SATURDAY 24 EXETER, UNIVERSITY SUNDAY 25 BRISTOL, FLEECE & FIRKIN TUESDAY 27 BRIGHTON, ZAP CLUB WEDNESDAY 28 OXFORD, THE VENUE THURSDAY 29 BOURNEMOUTH, HOTHOUSE FRIDAY 30 PORTSMOUTH, POLYTECHNIC DECEMBER SATURDAY 1 CANTERBURY, KENT UNIVERSITY SUNDAY 2 WALSALL, JUNCTION 10 TUESDAY 4 BIRMINGHAM, EDWARDS NO. 8 WEDNESDAY 5 SHEFFIELD, UNIVERSITY THURSDAY 6 LEICESTER, PRINCESS CHARLOTTE FRIDAY 7 MANCHESTER, THE BOARDWALK SUNDAY 9 CAMBRIDGE, THE JUNCTION

AIR CONDITIONED NIGHTMARE

Every Wednesday
DJ's: Mike Pickering
Jon Dasilva
Justin Robertson

Admission £3

Starts 17 October

FAC 51 The Haçienda

11/13
Whitworth St. West
Manchester
061- 236 5051

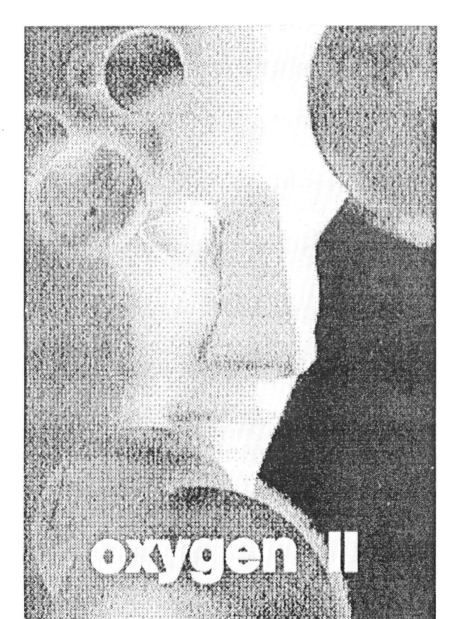

oxygen II

5 Lysergia suburbia

Kristian Russell

Introduction

This should not be yet another simple glorification of the 60s: I wrote this piece to highlight what has increasingly become a driving factor behind today's rave scene - psychedelia. Whatever it means - spacey effects, trancedance, underground unity and disobedience - it seems to re-occur time and time again.

After a period avidly collecting 60s music - everything from Hammond organ, 'cool' to freaky, garage, guitar solos - I rapidly embraced rave music. Intense, emotional, highly rhythmical and often instrumental techno not only resembled 60s psychedelia structurally, but also hinted at a similar drug exposure that originally inspired 'psychedelic' musicians of the 1960s. Listen carefully to the weird sample intro to the Raggatwins *Ragga Trip*, or the backwards looping of Apollo 440's *Lolita Ambient*, or the mellow mantra in Jam and Spoon's *Stella* and Primal Scream's *Dub Symphony*. These records do not simply sample from 60s music, but convey a similar spirit that existed on tracks like Jimi Hendrix's *3rd Stone from the Sun*, Pink Floyd's *Interstella Overdrive*, or the Doors *Light My Fire*. They use state of the art technology to innovate new effects and pioneering new forms of music through exploration and improvisation.

Techno might, at first, seem the antithesis to improvisation, with computer programming, sequencing and sampling (the latter eradicating the traditional need for studio musicians feeding off one another to create further). The beauty of sampling technology, however, is that it enables *any* musician to discover and incorporate

91

'mistakes' into otherwise tightly controlled compositions. Jazz always thrived on musicians being able to express unorthodox ideas around a tight rhythm section - an area which psychedelia also tackled through experimentation with studio technology. The creative side of jazz (challenging musical theory) and the creative aspect of psychedelia (stretching state of the art technology) seem to have collided within post-Acid House British techno.

Some say it's punk all over again, some define it as trippy psychedelia. I would suggest it is merely innovative music again. Exciting times! My time in Britain during and after the Acid House explosion brought me into frequent contact with rave culture and its members, enabling me to base my ideas around my own sightings and attendance at events. What I noticed at street level suggested a sizable cult following with firm links to a drug culture and a new exciting form of music - that incidentally shattered many preconceptions about synthesiser music and youth's 'fragmentation': including my own.

However, let us not take all of this too seriously; after all they are only records we are talking about. To paraphrase an Acid House DJ and artist, Baby Ford, a record is just a recording - if it moves you, it's a good record. Long live the 'one in a million', White Label 12" - the one so good you can't find it.

Acid House: A fluke or revolution?

The validity of Acid House has been openly criticised and discussed in the British media since its birth during the summer of 1987. Some commentators maintain that it was, and still is, a genuine expression of dissatisfaction by a youth culture rejecting the popular 80s ideal of a capitalist society, where individual success was fulfilled through financial (youthful) enterprise and profits at the expense of more humanitarian priorities such as the improvement of public welfare services.

Excess marketing of youth movements during the 80s often degenerated the cultural validity of each movement into mere styles and 'fads'. Stock, Aitken and Waterman are perfect examples of 'conscious' marketing, where popular trends are picked upon and used within a music marketing strategy. Popular chart acts under the guidance of SAW include, Big Fun, Sinitta, Kylie Minogue, Jason Donovan and Sonya. But there were coinciding media developments which helped to devalue youth cultures into mere styles: like the rapid spread of satellite television, particularly MTV (the latter started in 1980) allowing information to pass from country to country at an unprecedented pace. Steve Redhead, quoting Paul Virilio, has also picked up on this theory by citing a satellite broadcasted event like Live Aid in 1985 as a "concentration in broadcasting time. Broadcasting replaces urbanisation. It's a city of the instant in which a billion people are gathered."(1) The speed and efficiency of this improved communication process prevented the cultural implications of each youth movement being digested by outsiders, therefore rending each 'style' superficial and shortening its life-span drastically. As a result many 80s youth culture developments like the mod, ska, jazz, raregroove and 60s garage revivals were valid partly because of their novelty value and had life spans limited to the length of time they remained entertaining to the media. Acid House was initially dismissed by the popular media as a similar 'fad', but in time it has proven to be as innovative and influential as previous youth 'explosions' (rock and roll in 1956, psychedelia in 1966, and punk in 1976)

If Acid House aspired to reject all that was established and dated, it seems strange that it should align itself as closely to psychedelia as it did. Was this a recreation rather than a creation of psychedelia twenty years on? Most of the material presented here suggests the latter, but there must be some fundamental social similarities that link the two periods.

There was much reminiscence and romanticisation about the 60s throughout the 80s amongst the original generation who had witnessed the decade as seen in Derek Taylor's book, and the Granada TV programme 'It Was 20 Years Ago Today' (about The Beatles' Sgt. Pepper album, and society in general of 1967). Many of this same generation had, by the mid-80s risen to the top of the music industry (primarily) and thus spearheaded the marketing of various re-issues of 60s music either in CD form or in boxed collector sets (like the re-issue of previously unreleased material by The Doors, Hendrix, The Byrds and Beach Boys). In fact, the introduction of CDs onto the market from the mid-80s was crucial to opening up a nostalgic market, with many replacing their original vinyl collection with re-digitalised and upgraded CD re-issues. Dave Haslam summed up this process neatly in an interview with Steve Redhead;

> Why discover another Beatles if you can sell the Beatles boxed set in a wooden box at Christmas time? It's a paradox as far as the industry is concerned. They still need a product, a new product, but they don't want it to turn the whole world upside down. They're quite happy to be able to sell house music because they also own shares in Smiley T-shirts manufacturers, but they don't actually want Acid House to destroy everything that's gone before and start year zero with the 'Summer of 88'.(2)

The 60s were celebrated during the 80s with a number of 60s revivals in fashion and particularly music, with mod bands (The Jam and Merton Parkas), ska (The Specials and Selecta), garage punk (The Pebbles and Nuggets re-issue series, and bands such as The Fuzztones), psychedelia (Shamen and Rain Parade), 60s pop (Primal Scream) and heavy psychedelic rock (Three Hypnotics and Mudhoney). These were not major label initiated revivals, rather proof of youth being inspired by past successes. Pete 'Bassman' of The Darkside (a deeply 60s inspired group) views this potential form of imitation with caution:

> The economic, social, political climate of the 60s will never be repeated so I view the whole thing with a kind of reverence

and enjoy the relevant and worthy parts of it (but also recognise the not so good parts).(3)

Steve Webbon of the Beggar's Banquet label referred to this process as past styles 'conveniently' revived for aesthetic and commercial purposes only. Even though The Darkside prefer to use the term eclectic, many of the bands mentioned above were comparably imitative and were part of a general trend interpreting the 60s on a purist level, repeating past glories rather than deriving inspiration from them. This was no doubt also helped along by major labels renewing interest in the 60s by re-issuing old material in CD form. However, once these 'hip' revivals were discovered by the general public, interest was lost and the 'hipsters' moved on to something else that had not been discovered. Ultimately, these revivals were as disposable as some of the 60s trends themselves.

By marketing the 60s as a daring, pioneering and exciting era, a process of myth-making evolved throughout the 80s, catalysed by the media and record industry. But was this merely a large and successful marketing strategy or in fact exposing the frustration of not being able to produce and sell something original and contemporary (similar to the paranoia expressed by 1880s Victorians in search of 'true' Victorian art)? Whatever the truth, Acid House was a reaction against *both* - anti-yuppie cliches, like market exploitation and anti-revivalism. Acid House rejected established club culture based on snobby exclusivity (raregroove, for example) and major label 'hijacking' of successful youth trends. However, it never rejected the 60s itself, as there are a number of coincidental similarities between the formation of Acid House and the formation of 60s psychedelia (some social, some musical).

The main similarity between the two periods is the general repopularisation of psychedelic drugs (such as LSD) and marijuana. With the 60s being generally portrayed in a positive light, it is not surprising that the drugs that predominated and helped characterise that decade would be romanticised by those who had not experienced the reality of that lifestyle. Eighties propaganda against traditionally termed 'hard' drugs such as heroin and cocaine blamed these drugs as the cause of the comparable failures of the late 60s and the 70s (both periods of 'excess' and debauched drug abuse and sexual promiscuity). State sponsored television adverts bombarded the population with uncompromising slogans such as, "Just Say No!"

and "Heroin Really Screws You Up". Of course, these drugs do 'screw' the majority of users up, so these adverts were not total fabrications. However these ads deliberately presented a one-sided negative message to make the younger population feel more vulnerable by the presence of 'hard' drugs. With the emergence of crack in the American ghettos as a lethal alternative to heroin, along with anti-'hard' drug propaganda, during the early 80s, it was logical that most preferred to experiment with relatively 'soft' drugs, such as LSD and marijuana (which were also cheaper to buy). There was also a new 'recreational' drug, Ecstasy, which served not only as a novelty but hinted at, in its name, a far more pleasurable experience compared to the potentially addictive heroin and crack. As a 'dance' amphetamine it suited the music as well as the club and music eventually began to suit the drug. Logically a clubber was more likely to try a 'dance' drug than a harder and potentially addictive drug like heroin. Ecstasy was billed as "a safe psychedelic" and even as a yuppie 'designer' drug!(4) That psychedelic drugs were seen as less harmful options was not new. 'Pot', in the mid-60s, was seen as 'healthier' and more hip than whisky (a popular beverage before 'pot' arrived on the scene). As pointed out by Paul McCartney, in a retrospective interview:

> A lot of young people were knocking booze on the head. You'd go to a party and say: "God, whisky! How can you do that stuff, man? It kills you, you know?" So it was becoming very uncool. It was healthier to be involved in the pot scene. It seemed clearer, cleaner, more peaceful.(5)

Could one assume that heroin became a 'whisky' of the 80s, generally portrayed as a 'killer' rather than a sociable drug, leaving Ecstasy as the 'pot' of the 80s?

One should also point out that Britain was becoming more exposed to drug availability, with improved smuggling techniques and increased activity within Europe and abroad at British holiday resorts along the Mediterranean coast and islands. The emerging threat of AIDS as a serious killer disease from 1982 onwards (with America as an example) resulted in many preferring to experiment with Ecstasy - and its energy inducing effect - rather than threatening their immediate health with sexual promiscuity, despite the fact that Ecstasy - like most drugs - enhanced the desire for physical contact and sexual urges. As Phil Sutcliffe rightly pointed out in Q magazine, Ecstasy "arrived at a time when drugs were being regarded with even more trepidation because of the association between heroin use and AIDS".(6) Ecstasy did not seem to be part of the sleazy and unhygienic lifestyle associated with heroin. Ecstasy experimentation amongst British clubbers started on Ibiza during the summer of 1986, where clubs were open until five or six in the morning, and the lifestyle was contained within the clubs of Ibiza and London during the whole of 1987 and 1988 until it finally began to reach a wider majority during the 'Summer of 88'.

This drug culture was based on a new drug, a new awareness of the dangers of 'hard' drugs and sexual promiscuity, and was spawned in the atmosphere of a far more liberal Europe compared to Britain, where dated licensing laws still restricted night-life between the hours of 7 p.m. to 2 a.m. It had also been in existence for at least two years before it finally went 'overground', in a commercial sense, in 1988 - most of the previous youth movements of the 80s remained 'hip' for less than six months before they were discovered and exploited by business enterprise. The Acid House movement thus came out of a period of drastic international social change (AIDS and crack) during the period from 1984 to 1987. Political factors in Britain also played a part which suggested that British youth were accepting liberal European licensing laws and social culture more readily than before.

Both eras also promoted dance as a key to music appreciation. The psychedelic 'dance halls' were rock concerts where the audience stood freely in the hall and were not seated (as in the 50s). Sexual liberation and the 'liberating' effect of drugs made dancing an increasingly popular form of 'digging' the music. The beat/hippie philosopher, Chester Anderson, confirms this by saying:

> Dancing to rock music was a perfect illustration of how two people could do their own thing together....It (music) engages the entire sensorium, appealing to the intelligence with no interference from the intellect.(7)

Acid House was a movement promoting dance as a form of music appreciation (as in the Northern Soul of the 70s) rather than a form of sexual foreplay, which the 70s disco milieu had supported. By recognising the dangers of irresponsible sexual promiscuity (in an

AIDS context), Acid House presented dancing as a deterrent from the AIDS threat (with the help of Ecstasy as a dance inducing drug) and a way of rejecting the dated 70s notion of the disco as a 'meat market'. Both psychedelia and Acid House promoted dance for their own reasons, reasons that were relevant to contemporary social attitudes towards sex and drugs.

Acid House picked up on the new technology (synthesisers and samplers) that House, rap and hip-hop had based themselves around; similarly, psychedelia helped to introduce a wider variety of instrumentation (sitars, gong, flutes, etc.) and new technology (effects ranging through fuzz, reverb, phase, and whirlwind and multi-track recording facilities). New technology helped the music to progress into unprecedented dimensions: hence, Acid House leading to Ambient House, 'scallydelia', Daisy-Age rap, and Indie Dance crossover; 60s psychedelia, likewise, spawned music forms such as acid punk, acid rock, folk rock, heavy rock and 'Funkadelic'. One could argue that the repopularisation of drugs during each period helped to open musicians' minds and stimulate experimentation. Drugs and the availability of new technology in both eras no doubt has a part in the similarity of events and progression, but for those experiments to achieve success and convert outsiders it must suggest a wider social change rather than a isolated musical development.

This takes us to global issues outside Acid House and club culture that emerged during the 80s , which resembled international and ecological issues of the 60s. It is not just the problems that link the two periods, more the reactions. Band Aid and Live Aid from 1984-85, could be cited as the beginning of a quest for global unification which existed within the 60s CND and peace movements as well. Band Aid protested not only against the unfairness of millions of Africans starving, but also against the wasteful EEC food mountains and over-production - which were seen as symbolic of the wasteful nature of the developed world. This cynicism stretched towards food processing and manufacturers, with large numbers expressing their awareness of potentially harmful 'E' number preservatives, sugar content and monosodium glutamate in processed foods. 'Mad cow' disease, or BSE, again highlighted poor standards within the European food industry. By the late 80s, food manufacturers had to print and display the whole content of their products by law - many products were marketed wholly by the slogans 'natural' contents and 'free from artificial preservatives'. In fact, many reanalysed their diets altogether, becoming vegetarian or vegan: with new foods appearing to back this move up, such as vegan cheeses and meat substitutes. It was not a new move, as the following statement, by 60s hippie philosopher, Allen Ginsberg, regarding the hippies vegetarian diet, illustrates, "The switch away from the heavy meat eating Texas war diet (aggressive meat filled with the adrenalin of frightened animals)...."(8)

Anti-terrorism, drugs and AIDS, from the mid-80s could be seen as potential unifiers of the world (all affecting the First and Third World). Ecological issues (although predominant throughout the 60s and 70s) became increasingly pressing, with the rapid destruction of the Amazon rain forest, ozone layer, the North Sea, British beaches and rivers, and the inhumane destruction of animal species (Chinese pandas, African elephants, Burmese tigers, Blue Whales, etc.). As the dangers were so tangible, reaction was slow but generally positive (lead-free petrol, CFC-free fridges, ozone friendly products, and the improvement of recycling facilities).

The breakdown of the Cold War and the emancipation of Eastern European countries from communism in 1989 was yet another positive sign for the possibility of world peace. Even the Gulf Crisis has been cited as the 'Vietnam' of the 90s - again an obvious link with the 60s anti-Vietnam protest movement. All of these political and industrial reformations generally echo the socio-political developments that occurred during the psychedelic period (1965-1968). The incidents resemble one another, but as was mentioned earlier, it was the widespread response and reaction to these events that link the second half of the 80s to the social developments that emerged after 1965. As 60s underground press writer, John May, pointed out in 1990:

What we're seeing is 1968 replayed on different campuses, the students in Rumania and Beijing being obvious examples. There's the same generation gap between the people demonstrating and those in power....

He continues:

All movements expand and contract in a natural organic cycle. Changes are taking place now which are immensely profound, yet the media aren't covering them at all. What's happening now is like what happened with punk, yet on a much larger scale....(9)

From a British point of view, it is noticeable that Britain has begun to accept European culture at an unprecedented level, and Acid House has, in a sense, initiated and reflected this. European music and fashion was generally seen as subsidiary compared to British standards during the 'Swinging' 60s, with London considered amongst British youth as *the* centre of world fashion and music. This feeling of supremacy was revived by punk in 1976, and the initiative was kept up by Britain through to the early 80s (during the mod, ska, New Romantic and Goth movements). Europe followed English fashion indiscriminately during the 80s, seen in the late success of 'goth' bands in Europe, like The Church and Sisters of Mercy, which lasted well into the 80s, long after British enthusiasm over this form of music had died down. However, as American ghetto street styles began to infiltrate into Britain and Europe, the US became the leading force in setting trends and remained in that position up until the Acid House explosion in 1988. Acid House incorporated the 'Balearic' taste for music, an idea picked up from Spanish holiday clubs, where DJs played an eclectic assortment of music ranging from Mandy Smith to Latin salsa, to Abba, to modern House imports. This relaxed 'Balearic' ideal confronted the traditionally competitive spirit that existed in clubland Britain during the early 80s, where 'hip' status restricted the enjoyment for those who were not that deeply involved and limited the clientele at clubs. That looser atmosphere, together with the freer licensing laws and policing existing abroad, led to an increasing appreciation of what Europe had to offer the 'limited' British club goer.

Since Acid House there has been a remarkable success rate amongst European dance acts in making it to the top of the British charts. Italian House (Black Box 'Ride on Time'), German House (Snap *The Power*) and Euro-techno (Altern-8 and Kraftwerk), Swedish/Nordic Beat (Leila K's *Got to Get*), Belgian New Beat (Front 242 and Technotronic), and Yello and The Young Gods from Switzerland have all had considerable success. Other ethnic European examples include Les Negresses Vertes from France, and the Gipsy Kings from Spain, are acts which would have been unlikely success stories in, say, 1980. Acid House also popularised raving abroad in 1989 and 1990, when British legislative measures were imposed to restrict unlicensed raves (and licensed ones for that matter) with destinations as varied as Iceland, Amsterdam, Ibiza and Normandy. Finally, some have suggested that, with English football clubs being banned in Europe until the 1990-91 season, the only way to get abroad socially for football supporters was to frequent these rave events. UEFA's decision to allow English clubs to re-enter European competition was a fitting symbolic gesture to the changes that Acid House had helped to catalyse. With these developments in mind, it could be seen that Britain's youth was, to some extent, getting ready - culturally - for 1992 and European unification, abandoning, in part, a previous cynicism towards European neighbours, at least in terms of youth and pop culture.

What has been established so far, is that there are numerous similarities between the psychedelic 60s period and the formation of Acid House twenty years later, but there are many differences too. Some of these are coincidentally social, ecological and political but some are musical and related to a period of experimentation with psychedelic drugs. The 60s raised a number of arguments over the validity and positive role drugs could play within modern society. That type of enlightened thinking has reappeared in the aftermath of Acid House. *The Face* and other journals addressed the issue of 'smart' drugs and their positive potential, not as forms of entertainment and youth abandonment, but as a means to explore and stretch the limitations of the human psyche. Instead of using synthetic drugs, medics are currently considering the use of natural capabilities and perception. An agent like Piracetam has caused a minor sensation, due to its ability to channel a "well defined" flow between the subconscious and conscious. These medics are referred to as "new types" of doctors who are part of a trend, aware of the better sides to drugs and are, seemingly, willing to address the issues LSD and mescaline previously brought up thirty years ago. These 'smart' drugs are not just useful in psychological research but have also been used to improve body tissue and even defer the ageing process. Deprenyl is currently used in the treatment of Parkinson's disease because of its ability to prevent "free radical damage" (the long-term destructive/aging effect of oxygenation in the brain) and because it lengthens the average mice lifespan by a massive 40%.[10] These 'smart' nutrients effectively 'rejuvenate' the body but, of course, do have side-effects. However, the overall social effect could be a more general responsibility towards the use of drugs in view of the lessons learnt from the late-60s. Ravers have been known to switch to natural sources of energy (like Guarana and vitamins) in a conscious move away from synthetic stimulants (Ecstasy and amphetamines).

Musical and design statements made in the 60s and late 80s also relate to one another, sometimes repeating each other, but they are linked through the way those ideas were arrived at. Exposure to psychedelic drugs does not lead to the same results, as we shall see later, but depend closely on the individuals social conditioning, motives, and on the technology available. Acid House no doubt pillaged, to a certain degree, from psychedelia as well as other previous forms of design and expression. Psychedelia, however, also revived Victorian aesthetics and established music forms, but like Acid House, transformed these into modern equivalents that were relevant to contemporaries. Both eras were phases of drug-induced historical re-assessment. With all of these factors in mind, it seems that Acid House was not a 'fluke', it came out of a period of great social instability and transformation, the results of which are only in their infancy.

Sources

1. Steve Redhead, *The End of the Century Party* Manchester University Press, p.46.

2. Ibid, p.45.

3. From a letter to the author dated March, 1991.

4. Peter Nasmyth, 'Ecstasy: A yuppie way of knowledge', *The Face,* October 1985, pp.88-92.

5. Derek Taylor, 'It was Twenty Years Ago Today', p.93.

6. Phil Sutcliffe, 'The Selling of Smiley Culture', *Q,* January 1989, p.11.

7.   Jay Stevens, 'Storming Heaven', p.406.

8.   Derek Taylor, op cit, p.138.

9.   Chris Salewicz, 'Heavy Petal', *20/20*, No. 12, March 1990, p.52.

10. Mark Heley, 'Smart Drugs: Pill Power', *The Face*, February 1991, pp.80-83.

The psychedelic experience: Can you pass the acid test?

In order to gain a full understanding of how Acid House has used psychedelia in design, it is interesting to go through the varied reactions to the psychedelic experience first time around in the 60s, and the regional adaptions of psychedelia.

LSD-25 was first synthesised in 1943 in the laboratories of the Swiss pharmacy company, Sandoz, in Basle. It did not arrive in America until 1949, where it remained part of a restricted medical research project in analysing psychological states of mind, like schizophrenia and paranoia. LSD-25 was an extremely effective way of creating temporary hallucinatory states of mind that enabled doctors and psychologists to literally enter the same states of consciousness their patients were experiencing - obviously enhancing their ability to treat these patients through a fuller understanding of their fears. Even though it was strictly used for psycho-analysis, its testers included not only medical patients, but gradually, throughout the 50s, members of American intelligentsia and the beatnik sub-culture, mainly around Venice Beach in San Francisco, Greenwich Village in New York and Austin in Texas.

Although the beatnik culture did not experiment with psychedelics, it was already closely involved with marijuana through its appreciation and limited exposure to the bohemian jazz and blues world; which existed mainly in black areas of town, thereby restricting white beatnik access to those 'scenes'. As the beatniks considered themselves philosophers and part of the creative arts field, they naturally took to behavioural practises that would distance themselves from 'normal' society. 'Pot' was not smoked openly however, because that would destroy its 'hip' status - and it was illegal. "If you have to ask, don't ask"(1) as expressed by David Crosby (of the cult 60s group The Byrds) meant that, by asking if anybody had any 'pot' you potentially destroyed your 'hip' status, and also exposed those who wanted to keep 'pot' underground and exclusive. What is apparent is that there was a strong American underground movement focused on a couple of large cities where drugs were being experimented with on a fairly restricted scale in the late 50s. As LSD-25 got more publicity through those beatnik writers who had tried the drug (such as Alduous Huxley, Ken Kesey and Allen Ginsberg) interest naturally strengthened during the early 60s. As it was presented primarily as a mind expanding substance, which could only aid artistic perception and literary expression, it is not surprising that it appealed to the limited number of beatnik intelligentsia aware of the drug: for professional reasons rather than recreational ones.

But LSD-25 was not the only form of chemical to induce a psychedelic, mind-altering experience. Natural substances, such as the Mexican peyote cactus (containing mescaline) had been used by ancient Aztec tribes as part of religious rituals to enhance spiritual communion with gods. These peyote cacti grew around Texas, which explains the early experimentation with peyote around Austin after the publicity caused by Alduous Huxley's essays about his mescaline experiences; entitled 'The Doors of Perception' and 'Heaven and Hell'. As mescaline was a natural substance - distilled from a cactus - it decreased fears about the harm such alien chemicals might cause to the body. LSD-25 and mescaline were also still legal substances (even though they were not available through prescription, only for scientific research) again reducing fears about them. Indeed, America on the whole was accepting prescribed drugs more and more during the 50s. In 1955 tranquilliser sales for the whole industry stood at $2.2 million, by 1957 that figure had catapulted right up to $150 million.(2) This incredible increase suggests that not only was America becoming more used to the availability of drugs, but was actively consuming and accepting them as part of a modern post-war lifestyle. Even cough mixtures, such as Romilar-D, apparently induced psychedelic experiences if consumed in large amounts - teenagers, rather than beatniks, did experiment with the effects of Romilar-D. Cary Grant, the Hollywood actor, admitted in an interview in 1959 that he had tried LSD-25, which proves that, by the early 60s, the West Coast underground and an exclusive minority had come into contact with LSD-25. Jay Stevens points out the ease with which LSD-25 could be obtained around 1962:

> In a major city like Los Angeles, it was as easy to go on an LSD trip as it was to visit Disneyland. Interested parties could either contact the growing number of therapists who were using LSD in practise, or they could offer themselves as guineas pigs to any of the dozens of research projects that were under way at places like UCLA.(3)

But the drug was far from becoming part of the lifestyle of a new drug culture; rather, it was kept for special mind exploration sessions with purely scientific (in Timothy Leary's case, religious) objectives.

Changes were taking place, however, by the summer of 1963, when Timothy Leary was dismissed from the University of California for holding LSD-25 sessions with a greater regularity than was acceptable to the Board of Directors. From this point it is noticeable that LSD-25 started to lose its scientific status, becoming more and more part of an underground lifestyle and thus being expressed in the music and arts of that society - the 'Family Dog' folk music cooperative around San Francisco were an early group of artists and musicians to emerge in 1965. Ken Kesey and The Merry Pranksters, formed the year before to basically document acid experimentation through film and tape recordings simultaneously publicised the drug via a bus painted in noticeable day-glo paints, travelling around to those who were unaware of LSD's existence. Even though Kesey and Leary were independently presenting LSD for its scientific merits - to enlighten people - many misinterpreted their cause. LSD became increasingly a recreational drug.

San Francisco was already a city that had a strong underground beatnik community around the Venice Beach area which tolerated subculture of that kind. By 1965 its old Victorian quarter (based around Haight and Ashbury Street junction) offered large, attractive and cheap accommodation whilst providing an opportunity for the beatniks to move away from North Beach, which was becoming undermined by tourists and hangers-on. That community though was already changing under the influence of British music and mod fashion in 1964. They were no longer beatniks by 1965, 'hipsters' more likely, emulating the scene in 'Swinging' London and acquiring a taste for Victorian art and design (reflecting the influence of their new Victorian homes). The eclectic taste emerging in Britain also had an effect in breaking down rules of what design and fashion should adhere to - hence the popularity of Napoleonic jackets and the 'dandy' look in Britain around 1965. Roots were acknowledged too, by continuing to take music 'seriously' (like the beatniks had), by listening to folk and blues, and also celebrating their pioneering forefathers with 'Wild West' images and opening of saloons, such as the Red Dog. This led to a mixture between the 'old' beatnik folksters and 'new' exciting hipsters, based on British mod styles (from Carnaby Street). As real British mods also admired American roots music, this bond was quite logical. What bound these two strands together was LSD and 'pot', creating a new form of expression and lifestyle that emerged early in 1966, soon termed 'psychedelia'.

The drug culture that cemented the 'old' American roots with the imported British ideas was important as it unified members' objectives and experiences. What was this 'experience' though? The effect of LSD on perception is mainly optical but also creates psychological implications which in turn affect the rest of the senses. Retinal recording in the eye of colours is enhanced, enabling many colour combinations that would normally not be noticed, to stand out more clearly. A person would not usually spot all of the varying shades of green on an apple immediately, this would be carried out subconsciously and require deep concentration and scrutiny before these subtleties were acknowledged by the conscious field of the brain. Perhaps 15% of the information about the apple would be consciously recorded. LSD not only heightens the retina's ability to differentiate these subtleties, it also frees the 'filtering' function of the conscious field of the brain, therefore allowing the conscious access to a higher percentage of information normally stored subconsciously (that percentage depending, of course, on the strength of the dosage).

By allowing a freer connection to exist between the subconscious and conscious means that stored memory of past events and experiences are more accessible (usually when the conscious part of the brain suppresses the majority of, mostly irrelevant, stored memory). But as the LSD has, in a sense, 'liberated the policing' of the brain, by loosening the filtering action of the conscious field, the capability to imagine and allow stored memory to interact more freely causes some form of hallucination to take place. Hallucination may also occur through the intensification of the senses, obviously intensifying colour reception. This would explain why some tones of green on the apple may be interpreted as being luminous or sharper than they really are (also helped by the increased powers of detection that the retina in the eye has received by the action of the drug). Maybe the improved ability to detect pigments (and the heightened handling of those pigments by the brain) causes alien colour character and differentiation to be created by the brain, which in turn results in hallucinations. There seems to be a paradox between the improved ability of the senses, and the heightened ability for the brain to get confused by the abnormally large amount of information held by the conscious field (information which has not been filtered off for subconscious storage). Like in hypnosis, the subconscious and conscious are handling information in unison - therefore breaking down social conditioning which normally helps to govern conscious behaviour. By breaking down those restrictions exercised by the conscious field, LSD promotes autonomous handling of new and previously stored information - normal logic becomes surreal. LSD creates a kind of schizophrenic relationship (perhaps even a conflict) between the retina (as a sense organ) and the brain (as a decipher of the information provided), hence LSD-25's original use in psychological research to analyse paranoia and schizophrenia, where the individual does not distinguish between the difference of conscious and subconscious actions.

Vernon Joynson gives a good run down on the positive and negative sides to those chemical changes in the brain brought on by LSD. Good effects are summarised as follows:

...(1) a change in intensification of sensory impressions...with objects taking on great beauty and colours...attaining a new dimension of significance, (2) the ability to see the relationship between the many different levels of meaning and dimensions simultaneously,...(3) in a small number of users, a mystical experience characterised by a sense of unity with the universe.

On the other hand the bad effects:

...(1) the 'freak out', that is complete loss of self-control, characterised by panic, paranoid delusions and horrific hallucinations, (2) the 'bad trip', a more intense version of the former, characterised by depression, fear and anxiety...(3) the 'flashback', the brief return of the acid experience hours or sometimes days later.(4)

Most of the bad points stem from the inability of the conscious field to accept full autonomy of thought and response. Problems also arise out of impurities in a particular batch of LSD - which was and still is common when sold on the streets. Pure LSD usually provokes a positive reaction, with clearer results.

That was a simplistic explanation of a complicated psychological state, but it helps to explain the optical effects LSD has on the user.

Dimensions in space, either visual perspective or physical volume, become distorted by the brain's freer handling of the visual evidence. Much psychedelic art depicted central vanishing points and cosmic arrangements, like the Chocolate Watchband's album cover for 'No Way Out' in 1967. Hearing is often blurred into more drone-like patterns, caused perhaps by the autonomous way the brain is dealing with sonic information (a sense of nausea brought on by the drug - marijuana particularly - also plays a part in that). This also explains the Indian raga/drone effect bands such as The Byrds and The Beatles introduced during this period, through their experience of Indian sitar music and a wish to reflect LSD's effect on hearing. These, then are the chief effects of the drug, and a brief attempt to explain the psychological changes that take place under the influence of LSD. Once people had experienced these fundamental changes in the process of perception most reflected that in their 'widened' thinking (as Leary would have us believe) and expression. I leave it to Paul McCartney and George Harrison to underline the effect of LSD on the lives of 60s users:

It opened my eyes. We only use a tenth of our brain. Just think what we could all accomplish if we could only tap that hidden part. It would mean a whole new world.
(Paul McCartney).

It's shattering because it's as though someone suddenly wipes away all you were taught or brought up to believe as a child and says: "That's not it!" You've gone, so far, your thoughts have become so lofty and there's no way of getting back.
(George Harrison).(5)

LSD crept on to college campuses during spring 1966, a period when LSD was getting a lot of bad press - but also a lot of publicity. The drug had previously been used only by artists and musicians along with the psychologists and bohemian intelligentsia. Kesey and the Merry Pranksters had been active across most of California since 1964, but the masses had only heard and read of LSD; until 1966 that is.

Previous teenage preoccupations in America had been symbolised most closely in the surf music of the early 60s, along with ballroom dances often called the 'hop', where 50s frat and rock 'n' roll music was played. After the British Invasion in 1964 the emphasis changed somewhat, moving away from the teenie appeal of surf to the more serious, sharp-looking and wage-earning mod. Surf was soon out, and British-styled R'n'B garage bands were in - the dawning, in fact, of the first garage 'punk' movement. But this reaction was an initial one, as LSD became more accessible. Various 'Love-Ins' and 'Human Be-Ins' were organised around the San Francisco area throughout 1966, along with 'Acid Tests' initiated by Kesey and the Pranksters. A mysterious character named Augustus Owsley III began to mass produce and sell LSD, giving each batch a different name ('Blue Cheer', 'Purple Haze') to differentiate them. Curiosity was further aroused by the increased amount of reports surrounding the drug. It was reported that from March to December of 1965 sixty five cases of 'freak outs' (where the user overdosed physically and mentally) had been treated in the San Francisco Bay area. However, most of these reports were in fact not accurate, and according to psychiatrist William Frosch (of Bellevue Psychiatric Hospital in New York), only 2% of unsupervised cases of LSD ingestion led to medical problems.(6) The impact of these sensationalist reports was strong however, and it was estimated that by June 1966 there were 15,000 'hippies' living in the Haight-Ashbury area of San Francisco (most having been attracted there by LSD-orientated events, and also by Leary's famous advice to America's youth to "turn on, tune in and drop out"). San Francisco not only offered actual proof of a *real* cooperative movement, seen in the 'Diggers', who were a group of people handing out free food for those in need and those just checking out the scene. 'Frisco' really did appear to be a cooperative community rather than a capitalist city. Leary himself estimated that approximately 100,000 people were using LSD in April 1966 (Congress took that even further after an FDA report, stating the real figure at 3.6 million!) Language now reflected the drug experience with slang terms such as "far-out", "out of sight", "bummer", "cosmic", "vibes", "groovy", "freaked" and "dig" soon to infiltrate into the vocabulary of most teenagers. Indian paisleys, bells, beads, kaftans, and cotton shirts were now worn to reflect the interest in marijuana culture (other ethnic groups exploited were North American Indian headbands, feathers and jewellery; Chinese philosophical insignia, ying-yang, etc.). Even though the drug culture was not deep rooted, the large amount of bad press and mythical scare stories inevitably led to the outlawing of LSD in

October 1966, by which time it was firmly established amongst the American underground scene, and now also evident in Britain.

Britain had also harboured an early (restricted) 'pot' culture since the early 60s, amongst the bohemian beatniks and West Indian minorities. Even though Britain was, in 1966, the centre of the world's attention in fashion and design and music, it still did not have a substantial drug culture. LSD did not appear until 1966 and it was generally never taken as a serious psycho-analytical drug but more as a recreational 'fad'. As LSD was illegal as soon as the drug began to make an impact in Britain, it never had the time to infiltrate at the same rate as it had in America. Derek Taylor points out that "Had the Pranksters' operated within the narrower confines of England, there would have been a very swift move to check them".(7) So Britain did not have the same liberal attitude that existed on the American West Coast, nor did it really acknowledge LSD's serious psycho-analytical advantage. Media crackdowns on the use of the drug appeared fairly quickly late in 1966, so the movement remained very underground, accessible only to a minority. As the media had 'discovered' the movement so early it is almost certain that it lost a lot of its 'hip' appeal but was nonetheless pushed by the fashion and music industries (and later the tabloids) as 'Flower Power', giving it publicity, but at the same time spawning a great deal of cynicism and ridiculing. 'Flower Power' lasted through the summer of 1967 but was largely dying in Britain by the winter of that year. Various drug crackdowns during the summer, such as the convictions of Mick Jagger, Keith Richards and Brian Jones (all from the Rolling Stones), the commercial flop of the Stones' 'Satanic Majesties Request' (an attempt to follow the earlier success of Sgt. Peppers that summer by The Beatles) and The Beatles' naivete and well reported disillusionment surrounding their relationship with the Maharishi (an apparently manipulative guru) were all severe dents in the side of British psychedelia, which helped its quick downfall. Also, the lack, in Britain of a Vietnam and the black Civil Rights movement to bond the underground youth movement again shortened interest in forming a substantial (psychedelic) counter culture - America's underground, meanwhile, grew temporarily stronger by the unified protest against Vietnam. 'Flower Power' in Britain remained largely a fad with a limited underground 'scene' centred around the UFO club in London, and the two concurrent publications, *IT* and *Oz*.

British psychedelia seemed to rely less on party politics more on liberal creativity. This is apparent in the music produced by British bands from late 1966 to late 1967. Procul Harum's *Whiter Shade of Pale* , The Beatles' *Strawberry Fields,* and *Sgt. Peppers Lonely Hearts Club Band,* The Yardbirds *Happenings Ten Years Time Ago,* Rolling Stones *Paint It Black* and *Have You Seen Your Mother Baby,* the Small Faces *Itchycoo Park,* and Hendrix's *Purple Haze,* were examples of the experimental and imaginative, but above everything else, aspiring to genius song-writing within pop music. For those who have heard these songs, they all feature stark changes in tempo and harmonic key. Lyrics began to reflect the drug experience and became poetical rather than simply being based on romantic entanglements and teenage frustration:

> Purple haze all in my brain, lately things don't seem the same.
> I'm acting funny but I don't why, 'scuse me while I kiss the sky.
> Purple haze all around, don't know whether I'm up or down.
> Am I happy or just dismayed, whatever it is that girl put a spell on me.
> (Jimi Hendrix *Purple Haze* , 1967).

> You thought the Latin winter would bring you down forever,
> but you rode upon a steamer to the violence of the sun...
> and the colours of the sea blind your eyes with trembling mermaids,
> and you touch the distant beaches with tales of brave Ulysses.
> How could his naked eyes were tortured by the Sirens sweetly singing,
> but the sparkling waves are calling you to kiss the white-lace nets....
> (Cream, *Tales of Brave Ulysses,* 1967).

Compositions became more and more complex as pop moved out of outdated blues 12-bar structures, under the influence of drugs, with higher aspirations (particularly with post-65 Beatles and Pink Floyd). New instrumentation and effects were introduced, as well as samples of audiences, orchestras, backward tapes, conversations and ragas to form an altogether more eclectic assemblage of ideas. Psychedelia here was not particularly an attitude, more an awareness and open mindedness to enable more creativity. On the other hand, commercial cash-ins were inevitable, such as the Flowerpot Men's *Let's go to San Francisco* and The Smoke's *My Friend Jack (eats sugarlumps)*. This cheap form of 'Flower Power' was strictly chart bound and has not stood the test of time where quality is concerned, in contrast to the songs mentioned earlier (see Plate 8). The English scene degenerated after the summer of 1967. The UFO club - as the only centre for psychedelia - was really just an 'outpost' of the San Francisco scene. "All it lacked was a license, having to confine its sales to reasonably priced soft drinks and coffee and food...." (8) Its future seemed inevitably short under those circumstances. Even the Isle of Wight festivals of 1969 and 1970 were seen, at that time, as well short of the 'events' that were Woodstock and Monterrey.

America too suffered from the effects of media coverage during 1967s hyped 'Summer of Love'. As the 'hippie' movement grew away from its underground status towards a more substantial scale and goal, problems arose together with disillusionment. Whilst Britain only attempted to scratch the surface of psychedelia - using it more for commercial gain in psychedelic 'bubble gum' chart hits - America attempted to come to terms with the lifestyle psychedelia had spawned. The politicised hippies (termed 'yippies') wanted change in the very ruling system that they had used psychedelic drugs initially to *escape* from, not just because of Vietnam but more because of the destructive effect of capitalism on the human psyche and the environment. For a year, in 1968, most of these loose ideals were prevalent and relevant, and the movement remained unified by the general feeling of "us versus them". However, as the impracticalities of the drug culture began to be realised, opinions splintered and general dissatisfaction turned into doubt.

The Haight-Ashbury area had become over-populated by 1968. Estimates on the number of hippies that lived around the Haight area in 1967 range from 100,000 to 200,000. A drastic increase from the estimated 15,000 the year before. Derek Taylor stated that, during 1967 this previously peaceful area had now witnessed 17 murders, 100 rapes and 3,000 burglaries. This, together with the fact that the symbolic 'Psychedelic Shop' (opened early in 1966 at the start of the psychedelic period) and the San Francisco 'Oracle' were now both gone, hinted at the death of an era. Rip-off merchants and entrepreneurs (nicknamed then as the 'beavers') had moved in and undermined the authenticity of the San Francisco movement. The 'Diggers' themselves staged the 'Death of the Hippie' in October 1967, on the very streets of Haight-Ashbury where it had started in San Francisco. Most of the true followers of the hippie ideal had 'split the city' for the country communities, where they could co-exist with agricultural self-sufficiency and ecological harmony. But even this gesture was, in a way, as escapist as the psychedelic drugs, as the rural hippies were running away from the harsh realities of America at this time. One hundred and fourteen cities saw violent Civil Rights clashes in 1967, with 188 people dead and tens of thousands injured. Meanwhile, Vietnam raged on and its horrors were witnessed on American television. It was understandable that hippie communes avoided television and newspapers.

It was not just blacks, marines and the Haight that were dying. Many leading figures of 60s counter culture were now either in prison (Timothy Leary and Augustus Owsley III, producer of most of San Francisco's LSD) or dead (Martin Luther King and Bobby Kennedy in 1968; Jack Keruoac, Brian Jones, and the slaughter of Sharon Tate by Charles Manson and his 'family' of hippies in 1969; Jimi Hendrix and Janis Joplin in 1970; and finally, Jim Morrison in 1971). The 'hippie' triumph that was celebrated at the Monterrey Festival of 1967 and at Woodstock in 1969 was brought down to earth by the killing of a black man, Meredith Hunter, by Hells Angels (plus several injuries and overdoses) during an outdoor concert by the Rolling Stones at Altamont, California, also in 1969. All of these depressing events collectively shaped the end of an idealistic movement that believed in the harmonising power of drugs and meditation: a movement that had hoped that changes for the better would develop as a result of enlightening the whole system with that type of consciousness-expanding experiences. Drugs themselves had become victims of new, liberalised attitudes. They were either contaminated or badly produced. Those who have seen the Woodstock film may recall the continual warnings over the PA system of 'brown acid'. Stronger variants of (or cocktails with) LSD resulted in drugs such as STP and PCP ('Angel Dust') - these prompted far more frightening experiences and severe paranoia. They were hell rather than heaven. These were signs of excess becoming the priority rather than the enlightenment gained from an experience. This in turn naturally progressed to the popularisation of addictive drugs (cocaine and heroin) and amphetamines. Drug use had passed through three stages; experimentation, entertainment, to abuse. A form of escapism had in fact been promoted which was not related to the original ideals that Leary and Ginsberg had discussed. This extreme drug culture could not be integrated into the system and be 'lived' due to its very nature of distorting reality into apathy. As Tommy Parasite rightly points out, the 'hippie' icon was the Damaged hero - a form of escapism from the harsh realities of Vietnam and black Civil Rights:

> ...the Sixties was an era of Damage. Damaged heroes became our new icons, exploring dimensions of incapacity and chronic self-abuse that would eventually be travelled by countless thousands...most of them romanticised the Damaged experience, convincing themselves it made one 'heavier' as they continued to court their own cultural and personal wreckage.(9)

The 60s ended negatively, as most youth cultures seem to do. The excess in numbers and manner dilute the original cause. But are youth cultures ever cohesive? Perhaps one should not think of the youth cultures of the 50s, 60s, 70s, 80s or 90s in terms of the almanac span, but more as cultural eras where a fundamental ideal was expressed by, initially, a minority which was exaggerated into further conceptualised extremes of the original formula. Imagine a cocktail that successively loses its blend and becomes undrinkable. The 50s did not 'start' in 1950, but in 1955 with Chuck Berry's *Maybelline*, and Elvis Presley: lasting until 1965 with rock'n'roll, skiffle, Motown, surf, frat, doowop, Americana, coffee bars, high school hops and drive-ins. Similarly the 60s really 'started' in 1965 with the emergence of the drug culture and political/racial instability (hence folk rock, experimental pop, acid rock, Flower Power, progressive psychedelia) leading up to 1975, with 'blacksploitation' funk and Glam rock: both cultural 'eras' metamorphosised into excessive updates of the original ideals. The 70s 'started' in 1975 with punk (followed by post-punk revivalism) - but we mainly recall the early 70s which was really a gory offshoot of the 60s. If this hypothesis is correct, then we are currently edging towards the end of the 80s -

which 'started' in 1985 with the hip-hop techno revolution, with samplers, keyboards and concentration on dance.

Punk succeeded in fragmenting youth culture, however, and this fragmentation still seems to exist today. The emergence of a punk revivalist band called the Manic Street Preachers in 1991 may be seen as the first reaction against the 'dance craze' and House music. With lots of "rattled treble-high guitar" and "Paul Simonon/Mick Jones *(both of the Clash)* DIY tops with aggressive Leftist slogans stencilled on brightly colours shirts..."(10)   The Manic Street Preachers relive the Clash and the 1977 punk movement - glorifying the guitar (this time anti-synthesiser), confronting the 'hippie' and the older establishment. The fashion and music industry reflected those divisions in the 'style wars' that took place during the 80s in the national and Indie charts, and on the pages of *The Face.* Dave Haslam in conversation with Steve Redhead has discussed how the market changed after the punk explosion in the set up of the Indie (independent) record-label industry. Tastes were fragmented. There was not the same kind of unity associated with the 'hippie'/'yippie' movement of the late 60s. On the now defunct Play Hard label Haslam said:

> We (Play Hard Records) probably sell 10% of the amount of singles that Factory Records sold at the same time in their development. A successful single for us...had...a feature in NME, a feature in Melody Maker, a feature in Sounds. There were very enthusiastic singles reviews on the singles reviews pages. They (the band) were on Snub TV the day the single came out. John Peel had been playing them for two weeks. Everything was right for them to sell well...but it sold a total of 1,700 copies which is nothing compared to sales of an independent record ten years ago that had the same media coverage....It would probably have sold ten times that amount.(11)

This decrease in sales does not simply mean a lack of interest in independent label music, more a splintering of tastes, each specialising in a particular area of music and fashion, building from one extreme version to another. For example, trace the development of offshoots from punk rock; thrash to thrash metal to skateboard thrash to 'grebo' thrash to punk hardcore; New Wave to New

Romantic to goth; neo mod to ska revival to 60s garage punk revival to rockabilly revival to psychobilly to 'perfect' guitar pop to psychedelic revival. These progressions not only create new taste brackets but also leads to an extremely dispersed market, where individualities are expressed by developing established forms further to extremes. Youth is diluted by mixed, individual interests but united in the search for an ultimate form.

Youth movements are not necessarily unified (especially in the case of punk and post-punk) but the overall wish to reject all that is established and no longer relevant does unify youth cultures into a swift departure that resembles an explosion or 'youth-quake'. Acid House might have been the start of a reaction against post-punk fragmentation, with common experiences (80s Tory unemployment) and objectives (raving) uniting youth once again, like the 60s, in the form of a 'dance craze'. The lessons learnt from the failure to make sixties psychedelia part of a practical lifestyle have been learnt by a generation that have seen the dangers of heroin, crack, early 70s excess, AIDS and the greenhouse effect. Whether these worldwide problems are enough to unite everyone as one is another matter.

Sources

1.   David Crosby/Carl Gottlieb, 'Long Time Gone', p.36.

2.   Rev. Tommy Parasite, *The Boy Looked at Roky*, Pebbles LP, No. 7.

3.   Jay Stevens, 'Storming Heaven', p.242.

4.   Vernon Joynson, 'The Acid Trip', p.4.

5.   Derek Taylor, 'It Was Twenty Years Ago Today', p.99.

6.   Jay Stevens, op cit, p.372.

7.   Derek Taylor, op cit, p.111.

8.   Vernon Joynson, op cit, p.6.

9.   Rev. Tommy Parasite, op cit.

10. Stud Brothers interview in *Melody Maker,* January 27, 1991, with the Manic Street Preachers.

11. Steve Redhead, *The End-of-the-Century Party*, pp.73-74.

Acid House: N-Joy acid rock!

The reason why so many comparisons are being made between sixties psychedelia and developments since Acid House is mainly due to the emergence of Ecstasy as a social stimulant in British club culture during the second half of the 80s. Why should such a drug become popular in view of the amount of scaremongering regarding harsher drugs (crack and heroin) that took place within the media during the 80s? On the other hand, Ecstasy was being consumed on a mass scale - could it be considered a major contributing factor in social and musical developments that took place within the emergence of Acid House?

English clubland came into contact with Ecstasy on Spain's Balearic islands (particularly Ibiza) around 1986, basically as an amphetamine to keep the unaccustomed clubbers awake within the later socialising schedule of the Latin countries. The nightlife there rarely starts before 2 a.m. (when most UK clubs close). Ibiza certainly has a drug history, as it was a hippie island during the 60s and 70s (as were Kos and Crete in Greece, for example) and they still house a large contingent of original and new hippie communities. The drug stems back to 1914 when it was used as an appetite and sleep suppressant by Merck & Co., in Germany. It remained obscure until the demise of the late 60s LSD drug culture, and by 1976 was seen by the medical world as a therapeutic breakthrough as it produced that "vital and transforming factor in psychiatric session - honesty. And the insights would be remembered afterwards".[1] Even though the scientific world attempted to keep it secret, Ecstasy's popularity in America, according the the DEA, rocketed from a nationwide usage of 1,000 doses a month in 1975 to 30,000 doses for one city alone in 1985! It became a Class A drug in Britain as early as 1977, but was easily available in America until 1985, as it was still held in high regard by senior members of the medical research establishment. That might explain the incredible increase in its use in the USA between 1975 and 1985, but it was probably due to the way the drug was marketed on the street: as a yuppie designer status drug and as a 'safe' psychedelic (acting as an alternative to cocaine snorting). It was sold on the streets as 'Ecstasy', a name that promised more pleasant sensations and fulfilment than its other aliases - XTC, MDMA, Adam and Essence. As clean and effective as cocaine but with clearer results than the now outdated LSD, Ecstasy was a perfect method to switch off from the stressed business environment of the American East Coast. It even appeared in yuppie orientated soap operas, such as NBC's *Another World,* and in slogans aimed at the 'young, free and single' audience such as "Don't get married for six weeks after XTC".(2)

Ecstasy was obviously a suitable social drug as it broke down inhibition and conscious defences which also qualified it for serious therapeutic use, a use that LSD had originally been intended for. As LA publisher Jeremy Tarcher points out:

> It kind of melts defences....There is a lot of empathy, an ability to see something negative and understand it in a more compassionate way, basically to become more loving.(3)

It was not long before Ecstasy began to arrive in Britain on 747s and more articles about it began to appear in magazines, such as Peter Nasmyth's article in *The Face* in October 1985, who wrote about his experience with Ecstasy:

> Defences were dropping at a rate it normally took people months to achieve...I also seemed to possess an extraordinary mental calm, as if everything were on a very clean microscope slide...There was no distortion of the senses or hallucinatory tinge, as with, say, mushrooms. Rather a kind of winter's night, mugs-of-Horlicks feeling. It reminded me of someone's description of MDMA as the 'hug drug'.(4)

Ecstasy arrived during a period in the early 80s when the UK was increasingly beginning to look to black American danceability, and street-wise ghetto attitudes. This might explain why Ecstasy in Britain was strictly contained within club culture rather than appealing to an exclusive designer minority. The dance-inducing effect of Ecstasy (through lowering normal inhibitions), particularly when mixed with an amphetamine (providing an artificial feelings of energy), no doubt influenced this too. The fact that Ecstasy was 'discovered', so to speak by a group of DJs (Nick Holloway, Danny Rampling, Johnny Walker and Paul Oakenfold) and clubbers on Ibiza, during 1986, also explains why club culture incorporated the drug so quickly. The free and easy atmosphere of a holiday island, plus the presence of hippies, complimented Ecstasy's empathetic nature. The style of club culture there was less restricted to hip tastes and snobbery, preferring to blend together anything that was, simply, danceable (from Latin to chart bubblegum to hard to 70s soul to rare-groove). This supposed 'Balearic' spirit was born in this relaxed holiday environment and open mindedness. People went to clubs not to stand out (note the post-AIDS argument that safe sex equals no sex) but to enjoy the music and dance. Sheryl Garratt, wrote in September 1988;

> It's a swift and street-level reaction against the self-consciousness of the 'cool' designer Eighties...In the AIDS era, free love is replaced by expensive raving, the crowd is more likely to chant "Mental, Mental" than "No Rain"...cool has been replaced by sweaty".(5)

Most of the social and cultural changes that were taking place during the 80s have already been discussed in the first chapter, so what was Britain looking at in black American ghettos that was so appealing? The 70s disco 'tack' of denim flares, 'Jackson 5'-style leather and denim caps, silver-studded black biker jackets and rare groove music (danceable jazz-funk fusion of the early 70s) had already been revived during 1985. Even though it suited the taste of British club goers and DJs, and was a lot hipper than, say, later 70s Glam-disco (like Boney M and Baccara), it was not really a derivative of what was happening in the 80s. Seventies funk had, in fact, been part of a general stereotyping process (now labelled 'blacksploitation') of black ghetto culture which was very outdated by 1985-6 as expressed by modern hip-hop and rap. The days of pimps, jive, Hendrix lookalikes and loose sex were well and truly gone. People were subscribing from a form of escapism to past triumphs which, in a way, fulfilled the function of the club: relaxation and switching off from day to day reality. But American ghettos were simultaneously crafting very danceable and very 80s derived music in the form of House, rap, hip-hop and scratching. These were new music mediums produced by 80s musicians for 80s dancers. The lyrics were harsh and reflected tough, ghetto backgrounds - i.e. representing a regime of 'truth' - whilst the music used the latest technology (keyboards, drum machines and samplers) and its eclecticism and blatant use of vinyl music - heard in samples and scratching - reflecting the mixed racial nature of ghetto culture. The term 'acid' that Acid House took its name from refers to this process of stealing an artist's idea ('acid burning'). This sampling could, of course, be interpreted as yet another form of regressive use of past styles, but the new technology made the music sound modern and therefore relevant.

It is thus understandable that British revivalism seemed redundant and pointless compared to what ghettos in America were producing. This, along with the fact that the rest of the British music industry was simultaneously being dominated by American rock artists, such as Bruce Springsteen, Prince, Madonna, Tina Turner, Bryan Adams, and by American soul, MTV, as well as the above mentioned ghetto styles. The few British performers that did succeed in breaking through internationally, like Sting, Dire Straits and Eric Clapton, ironically compromised to American market tastes and MTV (this was before U2, The Smiths, Simple Minds and The Cure broke through internationally - but at what price some might argue). Lesser British acts proved to be brief luminaries, such as Duran Duran, Wham! and Culture Club, whilst others merely imitated American soul (Five Starr) and ghetto music (Malcolm MacLaren's *Duck Rock*). British revivalism and dependence on America during the mid-80s must surely have spawned a need to create some form of national identity by producing a street credible music and fashion style. The popularisation of Ecstasy and the 'Balearic' spirit could be seen as a British move towards creating rather than re-creating danceability.

Acid House developed within London clubland during the 1986-87 period, with most of the original Ibiza contingent opening their own nights in an attempt to import the 'Balearic' feel to London clubs. Paul Oakenfold opened The Project in Streatham's Ziggy's, his other 'Balearic' nights were held under the pseudonyms Spectrum, The Future and Miami. The success of the operation culminated in the 'Summer of Love' of 1988 in clubland London, so called because of its similarity to the cultural changes the occurred during the summer of 1967 with psychedelia. Dave Haslam has cited a good reason, apart from a conscious attempt by Britain to force itself away from its overdependence on American ghetto styles, why Acid House overtook American House in popularity during the 1986-88 period:

...hip-hop was not quite what the producers wanted because there was something about it they didn't quite like, the music

122

wasn't quite radio playable, the sound was a bit too rough and the things that people were saying wasn't quite right...there wasn't really a lifestyle to sell.(6)

Haslam spotted the difficulty in marketing an American ghetto lifestyle to a predominantly white, middle class, British audience the other side of the Atlantic. Additionally, it does not look like it was the drug factor that pushed the movement, as it has been estimated that only a few hundred clubbers were regularly using Ecstasy even as late as spring 1988 - although some novelty must have contributed to its attraction. The movement represented something more authentic, a true British response to American House, Ecstasy and the 'Balearic' taste perhaps? The 'Balearic' scene of London had developed its own music form and fashion attitude by 1988 with recognisable forms that the media could pick up on and exploit, but which simultaneously, therefore, threatened its demise.

Acid House music clearly derived from two American sources. Firstly, Detroit 'techno', which is hard edged and digitally computerised dance-beats - a complete contrast compared to the fluid, biological rhythms of traditional funk music. That harshness relates back to the late 60s when the violent Civil Rights clashes and the Black Panther Party stimulated an equally violent musical response, seen in the hard rock of the MC5, Stooges and gritty psychedelic funk of Funkadelic. The second major influence with Acid House was Chicago House (and its closely related 'deep House'), known for more soulful harmonies. Farley Jackmaster Funk had a huge British hit in 1986 with *Love Can't Turn Around,* which was a song based entirely on a bassy trombone sample running through the whole track. Both of these forms of music derived from unlicensed and under-age clubs in ghettos, where alcohol was not sold, therefore, creating a market open for drug pushers with punters faced with no other option than to dance. English raves were held at a later date (1988-89) in similar circumstances, with no alcohol or bar sales, leaving little option other than to dance continuously for 6 to 8 hours (resulting in a reasonable demand for amphetamines of some sort). Drugs of any sort would, therefore, be more likely to go hand with Chicago and Detroit House - as long as they prompted danceability. Most forms of House are based on a heavy 4:4 drum beat which is often used to create a repetitive and hypnotic effect. Ecstasy and LSD also promote similar sonic interpretations, so their effects fitted well with House music.

Acid House married that basic House formula with a willingness to test old and new equipment and produce different sound effects - inspired by the psychedelic drugs that some people were increasingly using in London clubs. The Roland 303 bass sequencer was capable of producing a contracting bass line which swung backwards and forwards in the mix and in intensity - quite similar to the 60s effect: phasing. When heard at a reasonably high volume with a continually flashing strobe light, its effect on the senses is quite overbearing. It is an extreme barrage of the senses. 808 State's *Flow Coma* of 1988 creates that kind of assault on the brain's signalling system. Human samples, such as the voice continually stating "elite" that runs through 808 State's *Compulsion*, are reduced to robotic repetition (Humanoid used whistles for the same effect in *Stakker Humanoid* in 1988). Acid House succeeded in dehumanising the previously soulful Chicago House by orientating itself around new digital instrumentation. Music was facing up to the very latest equipment and basing itself solely on those terms.

It is argued that musical development resembled the direction taken from 1965 to 1968, as pointed out in the first Chapter, in that it was prompted by the use of drugs and a realisation of the benefits of modern technology. Ian McCann defines the formation of the Acid House sound as linked mostly to the availability of cheap technology "...then someone accidentally used the Roland 303 bass machine on a record and acid is born. Since the 303 is lying around in every crap studio in the world, everyone can do it."(7) Maybe Acid House was reviving the old punk ethic of 1977, that anyone could produce music because there were cheap opportunities? David Roberts' description of the musical form suggests that it is indeed governed closely by technology:

> ...acid house pares vocal and melody to a minimum - substituting a mesmeric, repetitive beat as the central element in a swirling and disorientated collage of sampled aural debris, often including a wandering and gurgling bass line.(8)

Others have tried to attach direct psychedelic connotations to its hypnotic, trance-inducing quality which also appears in some psychedelic music. People did not just use lysergic titles like Sweet Tooth Sonny's *Acid Drops* of 1988. DJ Richard 'Noise' Norris (of 60s reissue record label, Bam Caruso) and Genesis P. Orridge (of Psychic TV) pushed the psychedelic connotations literally by using samples of 60s groups like the Electric Prunes on the Acid House LP *Jack The Tab* of 1988. Norris explains the reasoning behind the project, as an attempt to:

> ...create a new psychedelic dance music using the same aspects that I like about psychedelia - i.e. excessive use of technology plus humour and weirdness and pushing it to the limit within a contemporary format. I found the hypnotic elements, the trance elements, very reminiscent of certain psychedelic things.(9)

Norris incidentally defines an important part of psychedelia, the 'excessive' role of technology. Maybe Acid House was the ultimate form of psychedelia, in that it was generated by 100% technology? The fact that many danced tripping on Ecstasy and LSD led to similar forms of dance appreciation that had first appeared on a mass scale during the late 60s - due to the liberating effect of drugs and music. People now 'freaked out' to the music under the influence by standing still, keeping their limbs stiff and waving their arms, often shouting "Acieeed!" (this gradually became a symbol, rather than proof, of the fact that the dancer was tripping on Ecstasy). Others appeared more mellowed and slowly waved their hands in front of their eyes to witness the visual hallucinatory effect of LSD on the perception of movement. These forms of drug induced abandonment and dancing resembled the freak-outs seen in the films covering the Monterrey and Woodstock festivals of 1967 and 1969 respectively. But such conscious links to 60s psychedelia were rarely drawn at that time; it was danceability that became the prerogative, as DJ Peter Ford (aka 'Baby Ford', producer of the Acid single *Oochy Coochy (F.U. Baby Yeah)* in 1988) pointed out, "A record is just an emotion that's committed to tape. If it moves you, it's a good record."(10) What unites Acid House with psychedelia are its ethics. The hypnotic quality of the music and the media-labelled title does hark back directly to the 60s, but it was more the way it united a London underground from 1986 to 1988, and the re-analysis of psychedelic drugs, that relates it back to the issues of 1967.

Eccentricity developed out of the more relaxed club environment from 1986 onwards - a feature again evident in a lot of psychedelic music and culture. The 'Balearic' atmosphere that had been imported to Britain by Oakenfold, amongst others, was expressed by clubbers wearing tacky holiday style T-shirts with garish colours and naff "Surfers do it standing up" slogans. Dancers were reliving their holidays abroad all over again. Clothes were baggier, day-glo bandanas and straw hats were worn with sweat bands, all symbolising that people were not there to attract the opposite sex (although that never really ceased) but essentially to dance and sweat to the music. Alix Sharkey wrote in 1989 that the "...erogenous zones are strictly out of bounds....It is a retreat of the harsh realities of life. It is sexless, pre-sex, a denial of sexuality. It says **I don't want to get AIDS.**"(11) Dress adapted to priorities - sweat and movement. The gaudy, day-glo colour combinations were, incidentally, similar to the paisley patterns and pastel colour combinations that the 60s generation had experimented with - people were after all attending 'acid' nights. Some even wore original 60s dresses with flowers on them, or pastel coloured flared hipster jeans, all worn with beads, velvet waistcoats and Lennon-style circular shade glasses. Laser light shows at some of these clubs resembled 60s oil-slide shows that Pink Floyd and West Coast psychedelia used. Some even used original oil-lamps. The Shamen's recent *Synergy* shows in 1990 used original strobes and day-glo backdrops in an otherwise musically futuristic, techno-rave atmosphere. Another dance act, The Orb, incorporate films and slides into their live appearances in clubs, complementing their cosmic form of dance-dub music. Sheryl Garratt's description of the Whirlygig club near Leicester Square in March 1989 gives a good indication of the original spirit and the unifying effect it had on varying youth factions:

> The first impression is that you've walked through a screen and are now in some dippy hippie movie like Roger Gorman's *Gasss*, but then you see an unmistakably English crowd; against a soundtrack of ska, Latin and world beat tracks, aging hippies mix with New Man, African students, Goth punks who discovered pacifism and animal lib at the same time as crimpers, trance dancers....(12)

Not only was the club reliving 60s feel in the music and decor but was also reviving a San Franciscan ideal of 1966, in the 'gathering of tribes' - young, old and differing youth factions. Youth had fragmented in the aftermath of 70s punk, but was now beginning to reunite in the light of some severe sociopolitical developments. It was the spectre of widespread youth unemployment, unsuccessful youth training schemes, outdated licensing laws (compared with the rest of Europe), dilapidated public and national health services (a sign of the Government's refusal to take responsibility for social services) and the North and South wealth 'divide', that resulted in uniform political opinion within youth culture. This was helped by a growing admiration of better times (60s revivalism) and an appreciation of a more liberally governed European Continent.

These clubs also revived the 70s Smiley symbol which represented not only the tacky element, but also the joyous high experienced on an Ecstasy trip and full union with the beat of the music. The Smiley badge had a history in 70s dance music, again making it an appropriate symbol. A certain sense of youth unity was no doubt also a part of all that subconscious symbolism. However, these were tangible features of a definite youth underground, which could be identified and used to sell that lifestyle on a commercial basis to outsiders. Like 'Flower Power' in 1967 (and most other underground movements for that matter) Acid House went overground in the autumn of 1988. DJs D-Mob and Gary Hailsman's cash-in chart success single *Acieeed!* of that autumn killed off the movement's hip status and simultaneously arrived with tabloid mania regarding the dangers of Ecstasy (just like 1967s LSD mania) and Radio 1 banning all references to 'acid' on air and in the British charts. The hysteria dispersed the Acid House style but not the spirit - as suggested in the following chapters.

The first signs of a corporate push of the Acid House culture came during the spring of 1988, when Smiley badges and T-shirts began to appear on London market stalls in Kensington and Camden. Merchandise companies such as Pink Soda, CCC Clothing, Fans and Phaze were relatively quick to pick up on emerging club trends, relying as they did on younger employees who frequented the clubs themselves. David Solomon of Pink Soda refers to the Acid House fashion as "the strongest since punk".(13) Even if, by the summer of 1988, there were signs that the movement would be a temporary one, Pink Soda took it seriously enough and had already invested £15-20,000 in samples by July 1988, just to test the market.(14) By September another £100,000 was ploughed in to capitalise on Acid House. T-shirt slogans ranged from simple Smiley badges surrounded by "Acid House", "Acieeed!" and "Love Club", to more clever word play, like the potentially controversial "Turn on, Turin, and Drop Out", featuring the Turin shroud. Most of these slogans directly revived 60s underground slogans that had originally appeared in magazines like *Oz*, and *It* (as well as in posters from London and the West Coast) such as "Freak Out", "Trippin' Out", "Turn On, Tune In and Drop Out", "Wowie Zowie" and so on. All of these slogans referred to the direct, and side, effects of drugs, and served as reminders that both eras had seen youth coming into close contact with psychedelia.

Record sleeves became more and more anonymous, preferring to use plain graphic imagery rather than publicising the musicians themselves. This, of course, was due to speed of publication as many of the Acid House records were one-offs and issued to DJs only - not on general release. So the record sleeves had to be printed quickly and did not need any kind of aesthetic marketing. Most designs on general released records, however, had some reference to the 'Smiley' symbol on a plain, white background. One could see directly that it was an Acid House track by repeating that theme. 808 State's first few albums used a simple, digitalised band logo in yellow on top of a red background. The logo itself resembled that used by Adidas sportswear in the 70s, with three parallel lines forming the body of the lettering. It was very apt, due to 808 State's use of computers and perhaps was a sly reference to tacky 70s design (very 'Acid House'). Typography was also very simplistic, often resembling enlarged dot matrix computer printouts and sometimes venturing towards the futuristic, digital character mentioned above. Colours ranged from the ubiquitous yellow (from the 'Smile' symbol) to day-glo reds, oranges, greens and sometimes a darker blue. These were often contained within a thick black outline, giving all images a strong, informal cartoon feel. The simplicity and crudity of this form of record design is due to two major reasons. Firstly, budgets were mostly very limited (as in 70s punk) so designs were kept simple and cheap. Secondly, Acid House consciously wanted to break down the traditional idol-worshipping in music which originally came out of the 60s super groups (done to death during the excessive 70s) in an attempt to underline the music. It was not a new trend within dance music, as Charles Shaar Murray comments on 70s disco:

...dance audiences - in a spontaneous and unselfconscious

application of the 'death of the individual' theory - simply bought records they liked, no matter who they were by, rather than followed and supported specific artists. Successful disco performers were thus considered 'faceless' by a rock audience hopelessly mired in personality-cult.(15)

This kind of anonymity had also existed in many psychedelic record covers in the 60s where communicating the acid experience to the audience took precedence over the artists' identity. The 'trip' was recreated by extravagant, hallucinogenic illustrations. The Litter's 1967 *$100 Fine* had a pointillist cover where a dot printed photographic image had been enlarged beyond the point of recognition, displaying only wild colour clashes in dots of yellow, orange, blue and red. The back, incidentally, had a shot of the band on stage but silhouetted in front of a light show. Their identity remained unknown. Another 'acid punk' band, The Chocolate Watchband, had an 'acid head' on the front cover of *No Way Out*, a Victorian-glassed figure with his head represented as a sphere containing lines of dimensions. Strange purple clouds drifted across a supposed acid landscape with perspectal lines all leading to a central vanishing point, with the occasional interruption, such as a bush growing out of a squared hole in the ground. Grateful Dead had also used more mystical Eastern images in the *American Beauty* album in 1967. Chinese lions in red were printed on top of a sky blue background. A kaleidoscopic effect was produced by having a lion in each of the four corners, collectively forming a circular pattern with more mystical Chinese insignia in the centre. On the back the band had been photographed outdoors, silhouetted against some trees, through a circular lens not only representing a well known hallucinatory effect of LSD, but also rendering the band's members unrecognisable. They later employed Rick Griffin's strange imagery to decorate the front cover of *Aoxomoxoa* in 1968, where the hippie back-to-the-country ideal was presented through babies growing in the ground as seeds, etc. The psychedelic era wanted to portray the drug experience, whilst Acid House opted for even more anonymity, as the people who were producing the music were not in fact 'pop stars' (as they never played live or rarely gave interviews) but 'normal', streetwise clubbers and DJs who had access to keyboards and recording facilities. The emphasis was truly on music.

It is interesting to note that the British tabloids initially helped to publicise developments, but then knocked them down in a wave of anti-drug propaganda; a touch of deja vu as far as psychedelia was concerned. *The Sun* published fashion guides throughout September entitled "Acid House Fashion Guide" and "Groovy Cool, Lingo Guide". Their tone soon changed, the following month with headlines such as "EVIL OF ECSTASY" and "SHOOT THESE EVIL ACID BARONS". It withdrew an Acid House T-shirt offer in November. The backlash affected the capitalists as well as Pink Soda and CCC, who were forced to pull all of their stocks from high street stores (75% of Pink Soda's outlets!) Like Flower Power the original scene had been discovered and undermined by outside interests, and with that scale of interference from the media hype - and the police crack down that followed - it was inevitable that Acid House would peter out.

However, as in the 60s psychedelic underground, it was not just outside interests that undermined the movement, there was a fair amount of corruption practised by its fellow members. A dance fanzine and cooperative, *Boys Own*, later termed these Acid House and rave villains as 'Acid Teds'. Ecstasy was now being cut with impurities and being manufactured in extreme variants, such as 'Fantasy' (Ecstasy with mescaline, an apparently disturbing LSD cocktail). These drugs were now peddled at extortionate prices in clubs. It was mostly produced in America at around 50 pence per tab; then sold to wholesalers for roughly £2. By the time it reached British clubs prices ranged from £12 minimum to a ridiculous rip-off price of £30. But it was not just outsiders who were taking advantage of things - this form of, and instinct for, private enterprise had been cultivated within Margaret Thatcher's well publicised Tory ideal. Nathan McGough, manager of one of the bands associated with the (later) dance 'craze', Happy Mondays, picked up on this at the summer's New Music Seminar in New York:

...the whole kind of raison d'etre of Thatcherism and the political and economic culture was to do it yourself, get off your arse, make some money, get rich quick. For (people)...in their teens or their early twenties who didn't have the educational privilege or motivation to do a 9 to 5 straight job, or the opportunity to do it, or even the inclination to want to do it, and thousands like them from the British projects - the council estates - what developed was a mass criminal youth culture...the way that they could get rich and make their money was to sell drugs. When Ecstasy came along, very early on, you could sell it for £20 or £30 a tablet...and they were able to get hold of thousands of Ecstasy.(16)

Capitalist motives were once again causing disruption within the underground scene, which had also been evident in the demise of the late 60s hippie movement. An 'adult' capitalist 'system' had once again infiltrated and aligned itself within a form of youth culture, but in doing so had distorted and exploited this same culture.

Ian McCann highlighted the long-term danger of Acid House becoming primarily a fad which occurs when:

> ...someone sticks a drug connotation on it, millions decide that drugs are a fun thing, the raves fill up with ravers...Acid is a **sidetrack** that everyone is tricked along, and it does house no good whatsoever...(17)

Acid House and psychedelia are both cultural movements that suffered when the drug factor became increasingly predominant. This tendency derived from an initial confusion as to the part drugs played in these cultural movements. As these movements developed, under the impact of new musics and new technologies, they veered towards excess. It became distorted when members tried to build on new developments in music and technology, resulting in excess. The next few sections will deal with the aftermaths of Acid House, documenting the dance 'craze' in Britain that started in the summer of 1989, and its similarities to psychedelic design and music.

Sources

1. Peter Nasmyth, 'Ecstasy: A yuppie way of knowledge', *The Face*, October 1985, p.88.

2. Ibid, pp.88-92.

3. Jay Stevens, *Storming Heaven*, p.488.

4. Peter Nasmyth, op cit, pp.88-92.

5.   Sheryl Garratt, *The Face,* September 1988, pp.62-63.

6.   Steve Redhead, *The End-of-the-Century Party,* p.45.

7.   Ian McCann, 'Chicago, Chillinois', *New Musical Express,* May 26, 1990, p.22.

8.   David Roberts, 'The Grin Factor', *The Face,* October 1988, pp.64-66.

9.   Ibid, p.66.

10. Ibid, p.66.

11. Alix Sharkey, 'Cradle Snatchers', *20/20,* No. 9, December 1989, pp.56-57.

12. Sheryl Garratt, *The Face,* March 1989.

13. Phil Sutcliffe, 'The Selling of Smiley Culture', *Q,* January 1989, pp.8-12.

14. Ibid, pp.8-12.

15. Charles Shaar Murray, *Crosstown Traffic,* p.95.

16. Steve Sutherland, 'Wake Up America, You're Dead', *Melody Maker,* August 4, 1990, p.8.

17. Ian McCann, op cit, p.22.

Rave down: Whose law is it anyway?

The demise of Acid House during the winter of 1988 did not kill of the general appetite for 'danceability'; in fact it began to take over not only club culture but also music appreciation as a whole. The 'Indie crossover' and 'Manchester' sound will be looked at later but they were physical signs that even die-hard 60s revivalists had 'tuned in' to changes in club culture. The initial reaction, however, to those developments took place during the following year, 1989, when Acid House went public, so to speak, and started to move out of small, underground clubs to larger, mostly illegal, outdoor events; some of which resembled festivals. San Francisco-style outdoor 'Human Be Ins' and 'tribal gatherings' all over again - the same kind of buzz, unity and excitement. This was no doubt helped by the fact that the summer of 1989 was one of the hottest summers on record, but there was more to it than that:

> ...after you've been wowed by technology, lost yourself in the music, entered a dance trance and made a half a dozen new friends and all the rest of it, there's the biggest spectacle of all - sunrise.(1)

It was a continuation of the looser approach of the 'Balearic' spirit that had rejected the snob exclusivity that still existed in some clubs (particularly after the large amount of tabloid coverage during the autumn and winter of 1988) and served as an even stronger suggestion that youth were once again truly united in their ideals and colour. The same was said at Woodstock in 1969, but had the numbers involved become too large to successfully bond and categorise as one?

It was not just the police crackdown on these large scale outdoor raves that stifled the continuation of Acid House principles. It is probably true that the numbers involved had just got too much, and the amount of profits to be made from them attracted organisers simply there for money, rather than those interested in organising a good 'happening'. Tony Colston-Hayter was part of the Sunrise team of organisers who described the procedures taken to organise one of these illegal raves, and the costs involved. The Sunrise formula meant selling tickets at £15 each, with a telephone number on them which punters would phone on the night of the event and be given (by an answering machine) the first of a series of destinations, where more details could be found. This was to keep the location secret until the last possible moment, to prevent the police from finding it and closing the site off. No alcohol was sold on location and there was always to be tight security controlling the event (with dogs). Sunrise were one of the more reliable organisers, who took great care in producing quality rather than solely generating profits according to Colston-Hayter. He mentions that a normal event cost roughly £60,000 to produce. Average attendances were, by July 1989, about 6,000 per event: the White Waltham Rave in Berkshire reputedly had an attendance of 8,000, whilst one at Wendover near Aylesbury in July 1989 saw an attendance of 12,000 plus - the potential profits to be made from such a massive event, illegal at that, were quite unbelievable.(2)   It is not surprising that a major crackdown followed in the wake of such illegal gatherings, where fire and safety regulations, plus the large amount of unmonitored drug dealing and taking, was justifiably unsatisfactory in the eyes of the state. Developments had simply gone out of control, and complaints were not just expressed by the law but also within the rave scene itself - with cynicism being directed at the degree of corruption that appeared increasingly throughout the summer of 1989.

Peter Hooton of The Farm (a band that have benefited from the recent interest in the 'Manchester' scene, although they come from Liverpool) mentions the fact that:

By the time the Government brought in legislation, no one was going anymore. "Fight for the Right to Party" meant "fight for the right to be ripped off."(3)

The slogan Hooton refers to was used in a demonstration by ravers, and so on, in the centre of London in the spring of 1990, when stronger government legislation was brought in to prevent further illegal gatherings. Cynicism like that expressed by Hooton is understandable as some of the 1989 raves were badly organised and lacked a decent sound system. Even the **official** Reading Festival of 1990 was plagued by an appalling sound quality, as expressed by many disgruntled punters. Tim London of Soho, another successful chart dance outfit, turns more to the hype aspect of the whole movement:

Summer of. Love?...Summer of having a Good Time, more like!...I see the rave thing as part of a tradition of people getting down and getting out of their heads. All this b--cks about the E culture, it's just people projecting their ideas onto something that's always been there: mindless hedonism.(4)

That statement may be an attempt by a band to disassociate themselves from the rave scene altogether, or more like, distancing themselves from jumping on the bandwagon, cashing in on the commercial success of the movement. If London is right maybe there is a natural link between the 60s and 80s through youth's willingness to 'party'. As DJ Terry Farley of *Boys Own* (fanzine and rave cooperative) said:

Ten years of Thatcher's government has created 'Energy', 'Biology' and 'Sunrise'. It's the sort of yuppie, city whizzkid, "I've got a vodaphone and a Porsche, let's have a party" mentality.(5)

The raver as an extension of the affluent Thames Valley region who can afford the £15 tickets (and extra £15-20 for a 'trip') on a regular week-end basis, has a car (and can afford the £20-25 petrol to drive around the M25) and has access to a mobile telephone. Going to raves was an expensive form of socialising.

We have already mentioned Steve Webbon's (of Beggar's Banquet) notion of there not being a direct connection between the 60s psychedelia and Acid House, in his view the only connection being "lazy language" and a willingness to "pillage" from previous styles to further current ones.(6) Beggar's Banquet is ironically named after a Rolling Stones album of 1968, and its off-shoot label, Situation Two, specialised mainly in 60s revivalist groups, such as the previously mentioned 'eclectic' The Darkside, Thee Hypnotics (basing their image on the Detroit sound of 1969 - The Stooges and MC5), The Charlatans (named, coincidentally, after the original Family Dog house band, but who have been accused of sounding like The Small Faces - they have also been known to call themselves the 'Chocolate Watchband of the 90s'), and Loop (a band who specialised in noise experimentation, simplistic Velvet Underground-type chord repetition, and who wear black leather jackets and pointy boots!) Both London and Hooton have made justifiable points in questioning the simplistic links drawn between the 'Swinging' 60s and the hedonistic rave atmosphere. There was no 60s revival connected to the rave scene. Maybe Webbon represents the few that *admit to* re-marketing the 60s (like the above mentioned bands on his label) as part of a 'post modernist' freedom to render past statements hollow by re-stylising them into stereotypes as part of a fresh marketing campaign?

Hooton and Webbon's point stretches to the argument over the authenticity of raves. Raves were not a completely new thing, but in fact an extension of the original illegal wave of warehouse raves that had taken place since 1978-79 at Battersea's Mayhem, amongst others. Funk music had been played there to a black and white audience. The enormously popular Soul II Soul broke through commercially in 1989, but had existed through most of the 80s as a cooperative of DJs and acted as a 'sound system' at predominantly black parties, but also at mixed gatherings (such as the 1987 Notting Hill Carnival.) Were the outdoor raves of 1989 as unique as previously made out? Colston-Hayter hits the nail on the head when he refers to the importance of the outdoor rave as it "appeals to people who were scared of clubs before."(7) This explains why interest in raves and Ecstasy rose so fast during that particular summer. It was the 'event' itself and the adventure in finding the location and avoiding the detection of the police that attracted the bulk of people. A sense of an exclusive minority (or underground scene) fuels all forms of youth cultures, including 60s psychedelia. The 'events' themselves were spectacular in their scale and atmosphere, as Alix Sharkey vividly recalls:

...multicoloured beams flare and sweep across the thousands of people dancing in front of a large stage....The noise blasts across the field and far into the night. From the stage a small plume of smoke unfurls across the crowd, before wafting up into the air, like steam off the back of some great beast....Blue, yellow, green, white; the lights and music pulsate together, the bodies move as one, and for a second there is no distinction between shape, sound, colour, animate and inanimate...all those bodies moving as one, silhouetted by white laser light, thrashing through a haze of smoke, pummelled by turbo-sound, an endless sea of frenzy, an ocean of beatific smiles?(8)

The nature of these events were like walking into one big, extravagant psychedelic experience with the lights and blurred unity - who needed drugs when you could go to a massive rave instead? Like the Californian 'Be Ins' and 'Trips' festivals of 1966 and 1967, these outdoor events, in particular, evoked the same social sensations and sense of unity amongst those who had never originally been part of the Acid House scene in London.

The same dance ethic and style of clothing still existed, in that people wore everything and anything baggy but now did so on the streets outside of the 'acid' orientated events. Acid House gear was rarely worn on the streets, but was only seen in the clubs. By the end of 1989 street fashion was beginning to be affected by the dance 'craze', which had, of course, happened with Flower Power during the summer of 1967. There was a temporary move away from the tracksuits and baseball caps of American hip-hop, with baggy, pastel coloured long-sleeved shirts being increasingly worn with large prints of flowers and Yogi Bear transfers. These tops were worn with baggy trousers and dungarees, beads, flower shaped badges and brooches, hooded top jackets and sweat shirts, all designed to wear on a 'street' basis and which were comfortable for dancing.

There was also a North/South divide appearing through fashion during 1989, with the emergence of the 'Funkidredd' in the South and the 'Scally' in the North. The 'Funkidredd' raver wore expensive designer wear (Gucci tops, 'box fresh' Fila and Adidas shoes, white Levi's 501s, unbleached Peruvian cotton tops, ponchos, African beads and pendants, ethnic silver jewellery and Timberland boots - the latter retailing at £100 plus?) This form of lifestyle could only really apply to the people who could afford it - namely, the affluent South. It was not just the southern poseur appeal that pushed this trend though. A lot of it derived from the Afro-Caribbean communities around inner London who were now regularly mixing with suburban middle class whites, and were often involved in the organisation of raves and 'happenings' around London. The 'Funkidredd' seems to represent blacks in Britain responding to Tory policies during the 80s, no longer content to distance themselves from surrounding white culture, but now actually getting involved with society and showing a more entrepreneurial spirit - an example already set by white yuppies. Lindsay Baker defined the 'Funkidredd' attitude neatly by saying that "...they straddle the gap between raggamuffin and yuppie without making concessions to any upwardly mobile cliché...."

Jazzie B (leader of the hugely successful Soul II Soul cooperative) expressed a modern British black attitude in the same 1989 interview:

My generation of West Indian origin is the last of its kind, my children will be almost totally English. We are now living in a multi-racial society....The Funkidredds realise this, we understand this, it's the dawning of a new era. Black and white grew up together, we're compatible.(9)

Jazzie B described the move away from stereotypical racial divisions in inner city areas. Caron Wheeler (who had sung for Soul II Soul) brought out her *UK Blak* album - 'blak' meaning a new type of British black attitude. America on the other hand still displayed traditional friction between ghetto blacks and middle class whites through the rap of NWA (Niggers With Attitude), Public Enemy and 2 Live Crew. Friction also existed within black rap, with Los Angeles-based street gang rap acts criticising commercially successful black artists who, they felt, had sold out to white tastes. MC Hammer and Young MC were termed 'House Niggas'. In Britain ska had united black and white interests during the late 70s, but that close relationship had been a strained and temporary one. The rave scene and Acid House had begun to reunite multi-racial priorities through dance, challenging outdated racial attitudes. Jazz rap act Galliano's song, *Reviewing the Situation*, tackled the subject of race relations in 80s/90s England.

Blacks enjoyed the financial rewards of their business efforts but never attempted to sell out to the white majority, instead using their cultural backgrounds to enhance their image and market the life style more successfully (dreadlocks, ethnic beads and jewellery.) Whites responded positively to Rastafarian attitudes and clothing with many ravers wearing Rastafarian clothes, African jewellery - and there were independent label bands that actually grew dreadlocks, such as Jane's Addiction, Nine Inch Nails and Swervedriver. Even The Soup Dragons employed a Rastafarian 'toaster' (reggae rap or chant) on their tame, chart bound cover of the Rolling Stones' *I'm Free* in 1990! Reggae dub music later became an important ingredient in independent dance music during the summer of 1991, through producers like Andy Weatherall, The Orb, Jah Wobble, Primal Scream, and endless dub remixes which were often very un-dubby. A lot of ravers' clothing gear, however, was bought at hippie flea markets at Kensington, Camden and Brixton - some of it also came from hippie islands in Greece and around the Mediterranean. The reanalysis of black peoples' role in Britain incorporated the marketing of Rastafarian image as well as old hippie values of love, peace and harmony. "A thumping bass for a loving race" as Soul II Soul preached in 1989.

Up North the 'scally'/'urchin' wore similarly designed baggy, long-sleeved hooded tops, but with the names of popular Indie bands (particularly the ones from Manchester) printed on them and naff consumer companies (Co-Op, Subbuteo and Happy Shopper). Football kits were emulated on these tops by using bold horizontal and vertical stripes - as most of these Indie kids were avid football supporters (especially in Manchester.) Extremely baggy denim flares, green or red baggies, suede pastel coloured Kickers (from the 70s), old cricket hats and gold sovereign rings. It all glorified the early 80s 'Casual' - the working class hooligan who went to football matches and got involved in fanatical fights with opposing supporters. The 'Casual' was obsessed with designer names, and could be interpreted as an 80s style mod. Both the 'Scallies' and 'Funkidredds' admired designer labels and danceability, but made conscious attempts to separate the North and South of Britain. The 'Scallies' did so mainly to win back some cultural credibility and hip status from a South that had dominated that role through most of the 80s. Out of the two, the 'Funkidredd' was more hippie in its ethnicity, but as the 'Scally' revived the flares and scored 'draw' (marijuana) so both accepted the hippie lifestyle and went to raves. Previously clean cut soul boys and hip hop breakers suddenly appeared scruffier, grew beatnik/Rasta-type goatie beards, longer sideburns and centrally parted shoulder length bob haircuts. The 'Manchester' phenomenon will be closely analysed in the next section, but for now it is enough to say that both sets of people generally 'E'-ed it, 'puffed', hugged and went 'tripping' at raves, emulating 60s nocturnalist drug culture.

Clothes may have suggested a looser link between ravers and 60s psychedelia, but the design of rave flyers certainly suggested a dance movement dependent closely on psychedelic imagery and states of feeling. Sheryl Garratt, reflected on the nature of the majority of 1989's flyers:

> The flyers for these events give an idea of the attitudes behind them: elaborate, full-colour leaflets show cosmic, quasi-hippy

mystical images to advertise raves like 'Infinity', 'The Meaning of life', 'Humanity', 'Phantasy' and 'Live the dream'.(10)

Like the original 60s psychedelic posters, many of these flyers are now collected avidly across the country. The Haçienda club in Manchester hosted the *Shiva* night in October 1990, which was advertised by using an ancient Indian typeface and printed in black across gold and another version across a spectrum of reds, yellows, blues and greens. Shelley's, in Stoke on Trent, frequently used simple Eastern philosophical insignia to advertise their *Introspective* night throughout 1989 and 1990. Ethnic symbolism was used along with 'natural' symbols, such as suns, stars, chemicals, trees. Fallows Too, in Liverpool, advertised their Fantasia night in November 1989 with a Mediaeval sun symbol and solar rays; Stafford Riverside Centre's *Oxygen II* flyer, also in November 1990, featured a scientific dummy surrounded by 'cosmic' globes and had obvious druggy metaphysical and philosophical connotations. All of these flyers were produced in the aftermath of the rave explosion of 1989, and took on a visual language directly related to 60s psychedelic design. Even Manchester's The Basement advertised their techno underground night by using an image of a futuristic robot surrounded by satellite orbitals - truly cosmic and futuristic. It was also printed on silvery-red background (an adventurous technique) and they employed a specific company, Display, to carry out the design and printing of the flyer. All of these flyers and the laser light shows made these events, cosmetically, appear to have been derived directly out of psychedelic design but they also reflected the musical changes that had taken place since the 60s.

Rave musicians and groups' names and song titles now centred on either drug related subject or natural, cosmic connotations. Astral examples include artists such as The Orb, *A Huge Ever Growing Pulsating Brain Wave That Rules The Earth From The Centre of the Ultra-World*, Plutonics, *Tubular Bells*, Interstella and Sunrise, *Movement 98*. Hypnotism and states of mind were also represented, through techno artists like Hypnotone, Amnesia and 808 State. Ecstasy's energy effect on dancers was referred to in Adamski's *NRG*, Guru Josh's *Infinity*, KLF's *3am Eternal* - a rave crowd forever caught up dancing after hours perhaps? A sense of underground unity no doubt influenced Digital Underground's name and Adamski's *M25* - the road where most of the southern ravers of

1989 gathered in search of the nearest illegal rave. Drugs also came in to the stew through names like STP Experience and Stereo MC's *Elevate*. All of these artists emerged from the rave scene not as icons, but as contributors to a collective cause, hence Guru Josh's *Whose Law Is It Anyway?* questioning the police crackdown. These principles were similar to those expressed during the psychedelic era. The same drug innuendo and obvious references to the underground scene and drug effects emphasise that link.

These records came in sleeves that included a fair amount of futuristic computerised images, but always with a psychedelic sense of the bizarre and the visionary. They did not attempt to revive old forms of psychedelia, but were products of a late 80s parallel. Plutonic's *Tubular Bells* sleeve had a computer simulated, geometrically shaped 'Stonehenge' monument in red, blue and yellow. There is also an ancient Eastern religious/philosophical symbol in the design. All this is evidence of the raves' attempt to unite punters' appreciation of the ecology and universe as ancient tribes had done through worshipping elements of the earth and fauna. There was recent talk in 1992 of illegal raves being organised in conjunction with the Summer Solstice at Stonehenge. These ecological connotations had been used by psychedelia in the 60s. The Orb's *Little Fluffy Clouds* single of 1990 also used natural meteorological motifs by its use of a photo of a series of silver-lined clouds. 808 State were also keen to use spiralling cloud formations, as seen on the back of their American release album *United States*. KLF's *Chill Out* album had a photograph of sheep grazing on pasture. Their logo, comprised of a ghetto blaster contained within a pyramid, resembles a logo used by the Texan psychedelic group Spacemen 3. The image in fact, derives from Victorian settlers in Jefferson, North America, whose original design had an eye at the centre of a pyramid. The design has had psychedelic connotations since the 1960s, as it looks hallucinogenic and could be seen to represent the dimensional changes experienced by the mind under the influence of psychedelics. Hypnotone's album of 1990 has an eye within a square printed on silver coloured computer-aided graphics on plain white. This image loosely resembled the pyramidal structure discussed previously, but as Hypnotone were a techno outfit their image obviously refers more to cyberdelia than 60s psychedelia. Modern digital, computer technology was being used to express ideals that had been portrayed through similar visual language in the

60s, but now different means were being employed.

Ecology, paganism, ancient culture and ethnicity were all revived subjects, but executed with updated hardware. Even pop art images had naturally been updated, such as the Lucozade bottle on the front cover of Adamski's *NRG* single. Lucozade was a well known energy giving glucose drink, as in the song title: something close. to the raver's lifestyle. This contained the same kind of social innuendo behind, for example, Andy Warhol's 'banana' on the front cover of Velvet Underground's first LP in 1967 (the innuendo in this case being sexual.) Less important perhaps, but a notable trend, was the amount of novel word play employed by many dance/rave acts, such as *N-Joi, NRG, Phuture*. Many of these dance records were released by small independent record labels; some were just one-offs, so it was not economically viable to package the records with printed sleeves. The Acid House environment obviously still existed. A lot of hip status was additionally gained by releasing a record in a limited edition, promotional format only - a process ignoring graphic design marketing. These rave records were signs of a further splintering within the record industry, but not in the public's taste for danceability - as all of these releases were similar in execution and appreciation.

The rave phenomenon reflects British youth's dissatisfaction with the now outdated licensing laws restricting English nightlife, forcing it to a halt at, normally, 2 a.m. The Ecstasy trip and the raves promoted all night youth entertainment which was not being catered for in the UK. By taking the law into their own hands and using a bit of Thatcher-inspired business enterprise, 1989s raves provided a hitherto unknown unlimited nightlife. *The Face* had an article in August 1990 that recommended night spots across the rest of Europe: a Europe that has more liberal licensing hours. Shoom had already organised rave weekenders in Holland in 1988, which attracted 2,500 people. Other rave destinations have included Iceland, France and Belgium, proving that there was an emerging interest and acceptance of the opportunities abroad. However, it seems that it is the novelty of travelling abroad that spurs interest in those trips. In Britain itself the legally organised raves at Quadrant Park in Liverpool, and the *Raindance* all-nighter outside London did not have the same nervous buzz that the previous illegal ones had. Did that mean that the majority only went to those for the kick of breaking the law? Jon Marsh of The Beloved (another converted

142

dance group) mentioned the two-faced nature of the majority of 1989's rave contingent by asking, "where are all those people who were out raving last year? Probably back at the football." He also refers to the post-psychedelic dilemma experienced in the late 60s concerning the negative aspects of drug culture affecting youth culture:

> ...it does bother me if there's a whole generation of people so bombed out all the time that they don't actually care about anything else. The number of people I know that I can have a political conversation with I can count on one hand now - people have just lost interest.(11)

The whole rave question, in fact, is underlined with the political frustration of living within outdated British licensing laws. One could say that the Acid House movement progressed into a 'yippie' style: political protest, by carrying this out through attending illegal raves. The message however was soon diluted by the simple thrill of breaking the law rather than achieving political change. That political opinion might not have been expressed as consciously as the 'yippie' movement of the late 60s, but it certainly ended with a conscious political demonstration, carrying the slogan "Freedom for the right to party". Could one not compare that provocative expression by youth to the anti-Vietnam and student protests of 1968?

Sources

1. Alix Sharkey, 'Magic Roundabout', *20/20*, October 1989, p.44.

2. Ibid, pp.44-49.

3. Retrospective in *Melody Maker*, December 22-29, 1990, 'That was the year that was', pp.70-71.

4. Simon Reynolds' interview in *Melody Maker*, January 2, 1991.

5. Sheryl Garratt, *The Face*, September 1990, p.65.

6.   From a letter to the author dated October 1990.

7.   Sheryl Garratt, op cit, p.63.

8.   Alix Sharkey, op cit, p.45.

9.   Lindsay Baker, 'Funki like a Dred', *The Face,* April 1989.

10.   Sheryl Garratt and Lindsay Baker, 'The We Generation', *The Face,* December 1989, p.62.

11.   Sheryl Garratt, 'The Beloved: Is there life after 'Happiness'?', *The Face,* December 1990, pp. 70-73.

Scallydelic Indie-dance: Dead dead Manchester

The British Independent record industry flourished during the first half of the 80s in the post-punk milieu of fragmented youth tastes. Up and coming bands were either signed up by an independent record label (and then signed to a major label, moving up the hierarchy.) Alternatively, they started up their own company to exercise full artistic and financial control over their work. Independent labels such as Rough Trade and Factory were formed early on in the 80s and were the start of increasing youth entrepreneurship. When these types of labels began to be considered 'hip' and more loyal to inexperienced talent, major record labels set up subsidiary labels such as Beggar's Banquet, Situation Two. Steve Redhead referred to this period of New Pop as an era where artists attempted "...to control their own destinies to a greater degree than ever before." Redhead then gives the reasons for this new way of thinking: "They had ample notice of the 'scam' dominated record industry through... 'The Great Rock'n'Roll Swindle' ...and therefore were able to employ self-conscious business practises...."(1) This trend was very much continued by the dance explosion, with a host of new dance labels being set up, sometimes solely for one single release. Examples range from Shut Up & Dance, FFRR, Splish to Evolution - all catering solely to the dance market. The Indie pop market had, of course, existed before the 80s - hence the survival of 60s pop magazines *Melody Maker* and *New Musical Express* - but it developed rapidly after punk's shattering effect, as isolated interests could easily be catered for by newly set up record labels under the influence of Margaret Thatcher's Tory policies that encouraged youth business enterprise.

By the mid-80s the Indie market was filled with bands and labels emulating previous cult heroes, such as Iggy Pop and The Stooges, 60s pop bands and fashion, 60s garage psychedelia, Velvet Underground, etc. Many successful Indie bands - The Cult, My Bloody Valentine, Jesus and Mary Chain, Primal Scream, and Long Ryders - dressed and played retrogressively to an underground who responded similarly to this 60s icon worship. This 60s purism continued through the Acid House period, illustrated by previously mentioned bands such as Thee Hypnotics who based their sound and image directly on The Stooges and MC5 (their *Come Down Heavy* album of 1990 resembled The Stooges second album *Fun House* in its orange/red/black toned multi-photographic exposure.) Even instrumentation reflected the strict purism that operated at this level with old, original Rickenbacker and Fender 'Jaguar' guitars and basses being considered the coolest instruments to be seen on the stage with. Thee Hypnotics preferred the sound of their original 60s technology - even though it led to numerous technical disasters on stage.

The Indie market was becoming a revivalist industry, coined by the contemporary music press with slogans such as C86 (Class of '86; twee 60s guitar pop), Class of '89 (predominantly noisy guitars in the mould of late 60s heavy psychedelia) and Sub Pop (named after a new wave of grungy, hippie garage rock from Seattle in 1989.) One can only explain this phenomenon by the fact that the Indie market is predominated by young consumers who are 18 to 26 years old. This is an accumulative period in life when individuals concentrate on amassing knowledge of history (musical and social) and gaining technical ability on musical instruments. Originality comes only after that 'learning' process, so it is logical that the Indie industry would be filled with simplistic 'adolescent' responses to musical myths and past glories. A perfect example of that development from a retrogressive state to progressive thinking is Pete 'Bassman''s account of his musical career that started in 1982 with Spacemen 3, who concentrated on exploration but did so under the influence of drugs. They were not technically proficient but 'stoned' enough to produce 30 minute, one note, high volume songs which they felt at the time "didn't conform to anybody's idea of a good group we know, and so felt like we were pioneers of a certain sound...."(2) In fact, despite their intentions, Spacemen 3 were repeating what the Velvet Underground and The Stooges had done twenty years before them, not because they wanted to imitate those idols (although they probably were aware of them) but because the same conditions were in operation. They were young, 'stoned', not technically advanced but still in need of exploring, musically as well as mentally, through the help of certain drugs. That was in 1982.

Today Pete 'Bassman' has gone through the above mentioned accumulation of technical ability and musical knowledge, and so his ideals have altered in conjunction with that experience. He refers to The Darkside as an eclectic outfit, aware of historical influences and keen to be inspired by learning from them:

146

We really try to listen to the best of the music made this century (I have recordings from the 20s to the 90s and in between) I hope people don't see us as a revivalist band...and wouldn't like to be stuck playing one style. I myself would like to use technology and push into more contemporary styles...I'd like to think that we also are honest and uncontrived because of this.(3)

One of Pete 'Bassman''s posters uses a portrait of a woman from the 1926 film Metropolis (note that it was coincidentally a futuristic film) tinted blue and contained in a spiky star shape on top of a cherry red background - resembling some of 60s designer Alton Kelley's Art Nouveau posters in subject matter. The Darkside's record sleeve design does reflect the experimental aspects Pete 'Bassman' talks about. The TV screen style dotted circles and diamond shaped images that appear on their *Waiting for the Angels* single of 1990 was produced by taping a painting on video and then photographing it on screen. It was an experimental attempt and used "out of necessity because we didn't have the time." Their LP used a fish eye photograph coloured orange and black, but was again a bit of a 'fluke', and its effect not anticipated. The Darkside obviously are not voluntarily reviving 60s style, more a 60s spirit to explore and develop individual abilities. It is also worth noting that Spacemen 3 (which Pete 'Bassman' left in 1988) have recorded a House song, *Big City*, showing their willingness to try out new ideas and technology. The rest of the Indie market reflected the regressive accumulation of musical knowledge which would explain why it spawned so many revivalist bands during the 80s.

The music press were, incidentally, eager to help sales by 'hyping' many of these new bands, billing them as new musical waves and giving them excessive coverage. The much discussed, adored and reviled 'Manchester' sound came out of this Indie environment around the spring of 1989, merging the traditional retrospective Indie style with the new quest for danceability in music.

The reason for it being named after a particular city was due to the fact that a host of new bands were emerging from that particular scene. Stone Roses, Happy Mondays and Inspiral Carpets, were the first three to break through commercially - all having strong links with past styles, in particular psychedelia. The Stone Roses wore denim flares, baggy football tops, 60s Sassoon style bob haircuts,

147

drip-painted their guitars, played a mixture of finger picked 60s guitar pop and Hendrix style dance funk, with titles such as *My Sugar Spun Sister, Sally Cinnamon, Elizabeth My Dear* and *I Wanna be Adored.* Their guitarist painted all of their record covers in Pollock style abstract expressionism. *Sally Cinnamon* had a photograph of three bubblegum automats standing outside an old shop front (a direct reference to 60s bubblegum and twee subject matter - the flip side even had a still of a pony tailed girl from the Monterrey film documentary.) Happy Mondays were well known drug dealers who wore baggy jeans but had closer links to the city's hip hop, House and techno scene (whose followers wore skiing jackets and expensive trainers.) With Funkadelic as one of their main inspirations, they played a similar eccentric form of dance funk ('Madchester' and 'Rave On') with mundane, day-to-day lyrics (*Bob's Your Uncle* and *Wrote For Luck*). Their record covers were designed by friends at Central Station Design, who used images of well known public figures over-painted by bright colours that clashed wildly (all very Warhol inspired). Inspiral Carpets looked similar to the above mentioned, but had an organist with a distinctive pudding basin haircut, they ran slide and light shows at their concerts and were known to play 60s garage covers, such as *96 Tears.* Their graphics varied from pictures of light shows and dry ice on the single *Joe* blue and yellow coloured negative pictures of trees on the *Butterfly* single, to more abstract silhouetted drawings of church windows on *This is How it Feels.*

To say that these three bands were strict revivalists would be untrue, although they made their influences obvious. Rather, they were early responses to Acid House and raves' call for danceability as a main ingredient in music appreciation; with hints of psychedelia thrown in for marketing visuals. Most of these bands' personnel had previously been football followers and reflected the terrace culture defined as 'Casuals' in the South, and 'Scallies'/'urchins' in Liverpool, ('Perries' in Manchester.) Their previously regressive attitude was now changing under the influence of the rave scene. That dance ideal was soon coined 'baggy' in the British music press, as a reference to the baggy dress of ravers - and Mancunians in general. But with the music press pushing all three bands, and enthusiastically writing a lot of false praises of the overall Manchester scene/sound to sell more papers, the movement as a whole degenerated. In fact all of the 'Manchester' bands denied any connection with their counterparts, only accepting a coincidental geographical link. It was followed by a media backlash (aimed mainly at the rock star attitude of the Stone Roses, who stubbornly refused to cooperate with the music press and industry) and the inevitable 'bandwagon' cash ins on the success of 'baggy' music.

The 'Roses', 'Mondays' and 'Inspirals' were soon followed by Northside, The Charlatans and New Fast Automatic Daffodils around the autumn of 1989. A year later a third generation of Manchester acts had been built up, largely by the press, but also by the growing reputation of the Manchester scene: The High, Intastella, Rig, Paris Angels. It is ironic that similar hypes were later carried out by the music press, to promote the 'Thames Valley Noise' bands (Ride, Chapterhouse, Slowdrive, Swervedriver), a Bristol dance 'craze' (Moonflowers, Massive) and Liverpool's psychedelic guitar strumming pop (La's, Top, The Real People.) All of these waves of publicity are basically the continuation of the old marketing strategy that generate the bulk of sales within the Indie music industry: hip status. Press representations of the Liverpool and Manchester scenes often presented the artists with scores to settle with a music industry that tends to centre its attention on London as the capital of entertainment quality and quantity, dismissing the provinces all too frequently. As Peter Hooton of The Farm pointed out, "Mass proletariat culture, that's what The Clash were about, that's what we're about."(4) 'Scallydelia' (in both Liverpool and Manchester) was a challenge from the North to the North/South cultural and financial divide - the traditional notion of the working class North and the richer, middle class South. London's Acid House might have accepted the ethic of anti-hip, but both Liverpool and Manchester were still traditionally competitive - very hip orientated. This clash had also occurred in the 60s and 70s, when Merseybeat and Northern Soul respectively, momentarily challenged London for supremacy in the music industry. But that is not the main link to the 60s as far as 'Scallydelia' is concerned. It was the way that the whole Indie music industry responded to the success of the Manchester based bands who had 'turned on, tuned in, and dropped out' under the influence of rave and Acid House.

Charles Shaar Murray has theorised about an advantageous form of marketing - the 'crossover' - in relation to black artists selling out to white majorities.

In the jargon of music business marketing, *crossover* is a magic word. It refers to the process by which a black act, generally one already comfortably established with black audiences, begins to sell records to large numbers of whites.(5)

Could one not apply the same theory here when established Indie bands basically bridge the gap between the retrogressive Indie audience and the rave scene, through its push for danceable grooves within traditional rock-guitar compositions and arrangements? They are both 'crossovers' through their multi-racial character (Stone Roses type funky guitar imitating black 70s funk) and commercial advantages (the Soup Dragons suddenly dressing themselves as ravers, contradicting their past).

This form of Indie crossover fusing revivalist tastes with new danceability from the autumn of 1989 has already been coined as the 'bandwagon', which basically refers to bands that were previously very revivalist in their image and sound, suddenly changing overnight to gain credibility and boost their waning careers by wearing baggy jeans and tops, beads, hiking boots, producing psychedelic videos and dancy guitar funk with the occasional weird sample. In other words, old bands trying to market themselves through the latest trends to justify their relevance to a new, younger audience, as their original audience had moved on. There are four identifiable 'bandwagon' processes of transformation that have emerged since late 1989.

Primal Scream scored a hit with their remix of an old song of theirs during the winter of 1989. *Loaded* was produced by a band that had first appeared in 1986 as a 60s guitar pop band (reviving tastes for polka dot shirts, pointed boots and leather trousers.) In the summer of 1989 they resurfaced, transformed with a topical biker image and a garage rock album, influenced no doubt by a series of commercial successes scored by Seattle based garage fuzz bands earlier that year (Soundgarden, Mudhoney, Nirvana) in Britain's Indie charts. It is not surprising that the groovy dance single, *Loaded* was met with general cynicism. The video used blatant psychedelic imagery through the hazy purple and cyan shaded shots of the band, still dressed in 60s leather and beads. The B-side had a live cover version of MC5's *Rambling Rose,* in an attempt to keep links with their previous revivalist nature. As MC5 were a high energy rock outfit it was quite appropriate to cover one of their songs in a rave milieu -

maybe it served as a pun? The follow up, *Come Together*, in the summer of 1990, showed the band with shorter haircuts and rave design clothing. The video also used grey and black spiral motifs and grainy, blurred shots of dancers - echoing 60s psychedelic cash in movies. A year later they released an album *Screamadelica* , which often blatantly pillaged from recognisable artists, including The Beach Boys *(Inner Flight)* , the Rolling Stones of 1969 *(Stone My Soul, Damaged* and *Loaded)*. Other tracks, like *Higher Than the Sun*, mixed state of the art sound effects and sampling with dub reggae, gospel and direct references to psychedelia:

Hallucinogenics can open me or untie me,
I'm drifting in a spell free of time.
I've found a higher state of grace in my mind...
What I've got in my head you can't buy, steal or borrow...
I'm higher than the sun.

One could argue that Primal Scream had always been a 'bandwagon' band, as they had constantly updated their image to suit changes in trends. The Stone Roses and Charlatans had even been goth bands in the mid 80s, but it was not an isolated example of this kind of turn around in image in association with the rave influence.

The Soup Dragons were an outfit that had not enjoyed much commercial success before they transformed themselves into a pseudo-dance outfit in 1989, dressing themselves in rave tops, Timberland boots, beads, longer haircuts, and used cyberdelia and spiral motifs in their videos. Their dance hit *I'm Free* of 1990 used computer generated, heat-detected patterns of sodium fizzing water, which resembled some kind of explosive formation of the universe in its finished form. It also used a trendy Rasta chant (termed 'toasting') in the middle of the song. The cover showed a futuristic looking spiked ball (in fact a coloured negative of a conker) which had been used in the 60s futuristic design. Their subsequent album, *Mother Universe*, had spiral motifs and cyberdelia derived from their video. This was blatant opportunism in view of the Soup Dragons unpsychedelic history.

Primal Scream's *Loaded* also popularised the idea of bringing in rave DJs to remix Indie songs. A second form of 'bandwagon' was the remix. This was not just using hip DJs but also introducing the danceability ideal into their songs, simultaneously elevating the DJ to

151

minor celebrity status. There were numerous remixes of the Soup Dragons singles, *I'm Free* and *Mother Universe*. Other particularly *un*danceable songs were remixed by rave DJs, such as Andy Weatherall's remix of My Bloody Valentine's *Glider*, Vince Clarke's remix of Happy Mondays *Wrote for Luck*, DNA's remix of Suzanne Vega's *Tom's Diner*, and The Cure's remix album of their old chart hits, *Mixed Up*. The Beloved even reissued their originally dancy *Happiness* album remixed as *Blissed Out* in 1990. The motives behind these remixes and changes in marketing are disputable. Some argue that it is mainly financial, others argue that it is genuine. Martin Price of 808 State criticises it by stating, "If I were a friend of theirs and totally into Indie, and saw them betraying their whole...past, I'd be sick."(6)   Bobby Gillespie (singer of Primal Scream) defends his actions as part of a natural evolution in rock history:

> ...rock as a forum for teenage rebellion, has been completely replaced by House. Indeed, with rock artists supporting worthy political causes, it seems that much of rock has been **accepted** and absorbed by the establishment....Meanwhile, the Government and the police are determined to bury the House scene, branding Acid House raves as harmful to this nation's youth. What could be more rock'n'roll?(7)

Another similar way of tapping off 'happening' trends directly was to cover old songs in the mould of recent successes. Tarting up old favourites to sell them all over again whilst simultaneously launching the career of the cover artist. We have already mentioned the Soup Dragons re-launch of the Rolling Stones *I'm Free*. Candy Flip's cover of The Beatles song *Strawberry Fields* basically just put Soul II Soul dance beat with the original track - cashing in on the safe and tested drum beat formula for success, and using the original composition of the song. Its cover showed the artists in front of a red and orange light show (similar to light used by Soft Machine, Pink Floyd and Grateful Dead and a host of other psychedelic 60s bands.) World of Twist's *She's Like a Rainbow* (again originally done by the Rolling Stones) and Danielle Dax's Beatles cover *Tomorrow Never Knows* weren't much better lacking renovatory ideas. All of these artists marketed themselves in the latest rave fashions, but were not producing anything original. They merely acted as confirmations of either a chart formula (like Stock, Aitken and Waterman) or were puppets of a street fashion a la psychedelic bubblegum.

Other 60s inspired bands did appear on the Indie market and tended to use fashionable styles of dress and danceability to gain further credibility points. Ocean Colour Scene all wore baggy tops, straights, played funky dance tunes, had the right kind of song titles but, like the Stone Roses, wrote their own songs around past styles which were, once again, fashionable. Five Thirty had Stooges type long, centrally parted haircuts, wore tie dye baggy shirts, flares or striped hipster jeans, trainers or pointy boots, used kaleidoscopic light shows on stage, with smoke machines, Hendrix/Jam riffs and wah wah pedals. In a similar vein to Primal Scream and the Soup Dragons, Five Thirty upgraded their previously outdated traditional mod appearance with new technology and fashion to suit new markets. The front cover for their first two singles used tinted photographs highlighted by striking cyans or yellows. One single, *Air Conditioned Nightmare*, (potentially psychedelic in its bizarre title) had a pop art collage, which mixed 60s images with Eastern monks, American 'bible bashing' slogans ("Jesus Loves You" and "Drive In sanctuary"), political figures and Americana. The inside sleeve had an Aztec wheel with splats of paint, green and ribboning, geometric patterning, flashes of red at the centre (very electric) and blue and orange flames. All in all the visuals were LSD and ethnically inspired. The songs lyrics also resembled the mixture of the illogical and mundane paradox that The Beatles and Ray Davies of The Kinks were famous for:

You can communicate with UFO's,
but you still take the train to Westward Ho!
You can perceive events at other worlds,
but you can't find the strength to cure your ego.
Real horror show.
Greetings my friend you're the Holy Messiah,
you swallowed a bible and spat out a lie.
Mr. Churchill wouldn't like me,
(Welcome to the air conditioned nightmare.)
Is your second name Picasso?
(Welcome...)
Take a cab to Piccadilly,
(Welcome...)

Feed the pigeons while you're there.
Five Thirty, *Air Conditioned Nightmare*, 1990.

This kitsch approach to song writing and image production, collaging information for bizarre effect, resembles what appeared in 60s design. Five Thirty's designer, Chris Drew, admits to the literal 60s link:

> I think ultimately anything of an artistic nature draws on what has gone before it...it seems probable that today's teenagers have similar attitudes and tastes to that of their parents, the teenagers of the late 60s. Although teenage adolescence is a time to rebel against parents, I feel it is more a rebellion against doctrines than actual attitudes, standards and tastes. By breaking through these belief systems and restrictions set by parents, teenagers can now hopefully enjoy and express themselves in a more intense way than their parents ever did.[8]

Drew mentions that teenage rebellion is a rebellion against doctrines. If 80s doctrines and parental values were similar to those of the 60s then the nature of teenage rebellion would logically also be similar. After all the generation who had been part of the 60s, and helped create it, were now parenting the 'rave generation' - perhaps having an influence on their children's tastes? He continues to say, however, that the late 80s developments were only "'influences' and I can not see it in any way being termed as a revival as the mod and ska movements of the late 70s were."[9]

Similarly, other bands, such as Ride and Dr. Phibes, looked like 'bandwagon' bands who based their sound very closely on previous role models (Ride resembling The Byrds and The Cure; Dr. Phibes sounded like Hendrix meeting Pink Floyd), but Five Thirty, Ride and Dr. Phibes, although inspired by 60s ideas, did not resort to plain imitation. Their close contact with 'baggy' tastes in clothes may have helped to distract attention away from their revivalist nature. Most Indie bands had, by the summer of 1990, switched to rave fashions, forming a new genre within Indie music either to keep up the rave spirit of danceability (an obvious link to a 'bandwagon') or to maintain the 60s ethic of discovery (a less obvious form of revivalism.)

154

The final form of 'bandwagon' jumping could be seen in haute couture fashions, with adverts promoting 60s style bouffant haircuts for women, with locks hanging over one side of the face. A group of couture designers (including Katherine Hamnett, Duffer of St. George, Joe Casley-Heyford and Jean Paul Gaultier) also revived the adventurous mid 60s fashion design of Pierre Cardin and Andre Couregges in the early 1990s. Deee-Lite, Kylie Minogue and Danielle Dax picked up on this form of couture, 'discodelia', specialising in late 60s/early 70s tack. The videos for Deee-Lite's first single *Groove Is In The Heart* and The Creeps *Ooh, I Like It,* both from the summer of 1990, had various figures dressed in original 60s clothing in camp, Glam fashions, Afro wigs, gaudy 70s shirts and extreme platform shoes. Rap act Definition of Sound recently executed a similar video for their single *Wear Your Love Like Heaven.* All these colours and eccentricity were used for pure entertainment value and visual impact. Instead of using up to date computer initiated cyberdelia, like the Soup Dragons, Deee-Lite used original looking psychedelic imagery as a form of revivalist kitsch. This was all executed in a tongue in cheek and theatrical manner, but was also a form of deliberate escapism from the harsh realities of mass crime and urban poverty experienced in New York. As Super DJ Dmitry of Deee-Lite explains:

It's an escape into hope. We're aware of all the negative things that are going on, all the destruction and lack of justice for certain groups of people...but you can either dwell on the negative or you can try to concentrate on the positive and that way change the way people think.(10)

This eclecticism was also the result of the mixture of social and cultural inhabitants of New York, but does a cosmopolitan background naturally lead to eclecticism? New York has a history for the kitsch dating back to Andy Warhol's pop art; his design for Velvet Underground's first album had used a simple banana motif. Later groups, such as the New York Dolls, Village People, Sonic Youth, De La Soul's Daisy Age rap and now Deee-lite all capitalised on the camp and tacky - aided by plentiful stocks of paraphernalia to be found at Brooklyn flea markets. The fact that ghetto culture had produced sampling through hip hop would also support this assumption of eclecticism colouring New York's media. Deee-Lite's 'discodelia' was a natural outgrowth from the American ghetto environment and Britain's psychedelic past was an appropriate market for their music and image.

Betty Boo also introduced a more lighthearted form of 60s genre into the British charts during 1990, with singles such as *Where Are You Baby?* which parodied stereotypical 60s fashions and James Bond movies. The song also contained cheesy keyboard technology and riffs, again done to parody obvious aspects of mid 60s tack. Betty Boo wore original velvet dresses, PVC boots, pointy winklepickers, hipster jeans, pendants and beads, polo necks, white lipstick and had a typical mid 60s bob haircut with headband. Soon the majority of women wear wearing 60s headbands in the resulting 'Boomania' that swept through Britain from autumn 1990 onwards. Even couture fashion models and fashion spreads followed suit, as seen repeatedly in issues of fashion and youth culture magazines, such as *The Face, Blitz, Cosmopolitan* and *i-D*, during 1990. As Betty Boo and Deee-Lite both catered mainly for a dance audience one could assume that their popularity grew out of the public's new taste for danceability and freaky 70s psychedelia. Betty Boo had previously marketed herself unsuccessfully as a female rapper in *I Can't Dance* in early 1990, but re-emerged a few months later in her 60s mode. Deee-Lite were not particularly new faces on the dance scene either. Brian Nordhoff of the similarly chart based dance act, Electribe 101, puts it that the:

> ...corporate side of the industry is turning dance music into a fashion but the problem with that is, what's in fashion this week is out of fashion next...it's a music business not a business business, the balance is tipping the wrong way. It's becoming a marketing man's dream.(11)

The exploitation of hip, underground movements was not a new thing, as we have seen through 60s Flower Power and bubblegum pop. The commercialisation of psychedelia seems to have occurred yet again in late 80s Britain through the commercial ploys used by Betty Boo and Danielle Dax in the mainstream charts, and by the Indie 'bandwagon' dance bands. Whether these reactions to the dance 'craze' were genuine conversions to danceability, or only premeditated marketing strategies are interesting questions and calls for deeper study elsewhere. The success of these music/fashion trends confirms that the British public had, by late 1989, accepted the taste for danceability that Acid House and raves had previously promoted. The fact that raves and Acid House had existed within peoples' contact with psychedelic drugs would lead us to assume that the mainstream public had also accepted drug culture together with danceability. Does that mean that Acid House really was not just fluke, but part of a cultural revolution or were the 'bandwagon' attempts signs of the break up of the danceability wave?

Sources

1.   Steve Redhead, *The End-of-the-Century Party*, p.9.

2.   From a letter to the author dated March 1991.

3.   Ibid.

4.   Mike Odell, 'The Farm: It's the Rail Thing', *Melody Maker,* August 25, 1990, p.40.

5.   Charles Shaar Murray, *Crosstown Traffic*, p.84.

6.   Carmen Myers, 'Primal Scream: Trip it up and Start Again', *Melody Maker*, August 4, 1990, pp.42-43.

7.   Ibid, p.42.

8.   From a letter to the author dated January 1991.

9.   Ibid.

10.   Andrew Smith, 'Deee-lite: Slipped Discodelia', *Melody Maker*, August 25, 1990, p.44.

11.   Paul Lester, 'Electribe 101: Chaos and Control', *Melody Maker*, September 15, 1990.

Ambient House: A huge ever growing pulsating brain that rules from the centre of the ultra-world

During the early spring of 1990 Ambient House emerged as a term to describe the more ambitious attempts within the rave scene to progress away from the drugs related rave culture that had become so popular the summer before. Sampling techniques and keyboard effects were taken to extremes to convey a sense of cosmic and meteorological atmospherics, that had only previously been expressed in rave culture through linguistics, design and photography - note the astral, cosmic names and images described in the 'Rave Down' section of this Chapter. It came out of a popular New Age philosophy explaining the 'random character' of nature, and expressed by rave bohemia and is illustrated best by the well documented 'butterfly' effect of an individual's movement on the rest of events across the globe. One decision and action has an exponential impact altering the actions of others. The individual may seem as inconsequential as a butterfly but in fact has an enormous incidental influence over world events:

> It is a holistic philosophy, which presents the planet as an interlinked structure. This means that anything that you do has a profound effect on the rest of the planet.(1)

A similar appreciation of earth's cosmic unity had also been expressed by 60s hippie intelligentsia. As these ideas originated from 'trip' experiences it is not surprising to find that Ambient House's peaceful, soothing and explorative character relate it almost directly to the truly psychedelic music of Pink Floyd and Hendrix's 1968 number *1983...A Merman I Should Turn To Be,* and George Clinton's cosmic funk freakouts of the early 70s, as expressed through his two groups Funkadelic/Parliament. Traditional House drum beats and piano riffs were replaced by transcendental 'sonic' effects to emulate emotional responses originally experienced through drugs like LSD, Ecstasy and marijuana. One could see it as the 'classical' music of the 90s, in the way it used the latest technology (which Classical composers , of course, did in their time) to orchestrate layers of melodies and sound effects (often sampled directly from the environment) with compositions resembling suites rather than songs, often running for thirty minutes or more. Its uncommerciality also reflects the intellectual bohemia, people today labelled 'zippies', surrounding its inauguration who are currently questioning the value of 'smart' drugs (natural stimulants and proteins) and investigating the limits of the very latest technology. Ambient House and 'zippies' represent an *awareness* of both the positive and negative aspects of drugs and computer technology, and could be the first signs of a culture in the twentieth century at last fully accepting the (New) Computer Age as a livable reality.

Before mentioning the 'zippies' and latest gadgets to emerge from the Western world let us look at the latent psychedelic connotations and ambition to be found within Ambient House music and design. KLF's *Chill Out* album of early 1990 is currently being cited as the first recorded output of a genre now referred to as Ambient House. The whole album contained two sides with no traditional gaps between songs (although there are differently titled sections on each side.) Recognisable House patterns, but with beats slowed down or very low in the mix, still formed the structure of songs but together with extended sampling of cars, slide guitars, radio broadcasts, speeches, crickets and other atmospheric 'sonic' effects. Like rap and hip hop sampling had previously been seen as direct forms of eclecticism, this recording extended the term eclecticism to daily environmental noises and rhythms. Samples were no longer there solely for cosmetic purposes but were integral frames in the songs' structures. The sleeve showed grazing sheep and pastures, referring to the ecological appreciation that had grown out of the rave movement in 1989 - visually repeating the back to nature covers of past hippie bands, such as Buffalo Springfield's eponymous first album, Quicksilver Messenger Service's *Shady Grove,* most of Traffic's LPs and Crosby, Stills, Nash and Young's *Deja Vu.* By entitling it *Chill Out* KLF were encouraging the listener to relax, lower their defences and preconceptions, and appreciate music as autonomously as dancing but with less energy (the term chill out also refers to the 'come down' effect from a 'trip' and ravers winding down at dawn after an all nighter somewhere.) There were also 'chill out' rooms, such as The Land of Oz in London's Heaven club, where weary dancers could sit down for a while and rest. In other words, the *Chill Out* album/concept resembled 'dance' as a form of *total involvement* with the music. In a sense it could be viewed as a 'trip' but a healthy one, as it was not drug induced.

The *Space Album* followed it later in 1990, and dealt further with the cosmic elements contained in Ambient House and drug imitated states. Its cover showed planet earth and other planets, galaxies, space crafts, astronauts, and contained continual references to Apollo missions through recordings of transitted communication between the astronauts and ground control. Other novel examples, such as children looking through telescopes at the stars again added to the trippy, spacey feel of the album. Much of the music resembled orchestral soundtracks for well known space films, such as *Star Wars, 2001* and *Superman*, but wholly synthesiser generated. The KLF's Jimmy Cauty collaborated on the *Space Album* with Alex Paterson, aka The Orb, who was responsible, in 1990, for the memorable *A Huge Ever Growing Pulsating Brain That Rules From the Centre of the Ultra-World*. This one song lasted originally for 20-30 minutes and contained an ode to Minnie Ripperton's *Loving You* (a psychedelic soul singer from the early 70s.) In fact, most of it comprised a repetitive synthesiser runs (in the traditional mode of House music) that were not particularly related to *Loving You* but without beats and a predominance of powerful samples, such as the sound of fighter jets rumbling. The Ripperton section was played through a lot of reverb making the original tune almost inaudible but creating considerably spacey depth. Other Orb tracks contained a wide range of samples, such as the jazz musician Rickie Lee Jones reminiscing about cloud formations and 'purple and red' skies *(Little Fluffy Clouds)*, plunging sounds made by an object being dropped into water, Apollo II conversations *(Backside of the Moon)*, Gregorian chants and anonymous speeches. Paterson does not take his music too seriously however, but is aware of its forward thinking:

There's been such a long rest after punk and nobody seems to have carried that progressive music from the 70s over to the 90 in any shape....The ambient sides you can go off and cook a dinner and listen to it, or water the plants or make love to....Whether it's the missing link after Pink Floyd, I dunno...(2)

Alex Paterson of The Orb has also been an important character behind the popularisation of dub reggae within dance music, in association with Primal Scream's producer, Andy Weatherall, Jah Wobble (former bassist with PIL) and On-U Sound records (a label specialising over the past decade with dub techno and traditional reggae/dub.) Dub music originated in Jamaica as a cheap form of producing B-sides to singles. By simply swelling out the instrumentation with studio effects and eliminating the vocals used on the A side, producers avoided the expensive cost of extra studio and session recording time. The result is a form of reggae concentrating mainly on the music (linking it directly with dance music and its ideal of entrancing the listener by sheer rhythm.) Dub thus derives from experimentation with studio technology, which psychedelia in the 60s and Acid House also encouraged. Rastafarian culture and religion additionally accepts marijuana as part of meditation and gaining inspiration, so one could also conclude that dub psychedelia and Acid House derive from definable drug cultures, and a will to fully utilise studio technology and sound effects. The end products share similar characteristics in shaping songs around a constant, hypnotic rhythm with spatious (arguably drug inspired) effects and minimised vocals.

Indeed the dance culture in post-Acid House Britain has readily embraced the close similarity of dub to modern dance music as described above. Successful crossover attempts between the dub and techno. All feature rip roaring bass, spaced out keyboards, generally bizarre but inventive samples, Rastafarian chants and slowed down hip hop break beats. These crossovers appeared from mid-1991, with Andy Weatherall's *DJB Symphony* (starring Jah Wobble and Primal Scream), The Orb's *Towers of Dub* EP, Jah Wobble's *Bomba,* and *Visions of You.*

Hardcore techno have also begun to experiment with mixing slowed down gangha rhythms with in time, up tempo hip hop break beats, as heard in the Ragga Twins *18" Speaker, Spliffhead* and *Wipe the Needle,* the Beastie Boys *Funky Boss* and Shut Up and Dance's LP *Death is not the End.* Even though this is very uncommercial music it has gained considerable credit for its pioneering spirit - the same has been said of psychedelia and Acid House. Shut Up and Dance reached No. 2 in the charts, in June 1992, with *Raving I'm Raving* and Future Sound of London/Weatherall *Papua New Guinea,* featuring a deep bass line, cosmic backward effects and re-verbed ethnic chants, also reached the Top 20. This is proof that a considerable number within the current dance scene in Britain appreciate and value experimental dub techno, although it doesn't dominate playlists at raves.

A number of independent bands have become popular since 1990 by sharing the same features as some of the above mentioned dance music. The Moonflowers use heavy bass, loose but fluid lead guitar, a mass of spacey effects within a general dance groove. Tracks like *Fire, Groove Power* and *Dub,* are not dub techno but display a will to originality (particularly in the lead instrumentation), elements of Hendrix, funkadelic, loose jazz improvisation and dub reggae. Not surprising, perhaps, for a band who perform dressed up in freaky clothing (or often semi-nude) and with Flower Power body painting. Verve are another group not sounding too dissimilar to The Moonflowers, displaying a tendency towards lengthy guitar orientated music. Many songs stretch to 10 minutes, but are released as the A-side of singles all the same. Levitation are another group hailed as being highly improvisational, with songs weaving and changing into progressive jams. Originality and experimentation unites all of these highly disparate groups; from the challenging techno of Urban Shakedown to some of Levitations 10 minute epics. Whether they have inspired each other is questionable (a thrash group, Jacob's Mouse, cite the dub techno of Depth Charge as a major influence on their music.) What is apparent is an underground youth culture that admires originality and extremes within any form of music, but currently, mainly music closely related to the extremes within psychedelia and Acid House.

The effect of this pioneering and fairly mind expanding music was aptly put by Colin Angus of The Shamen (another important techno outfit) in 1990:

> We like to think that the age of the sampler, and computer sequencing has opened up whole new veins in music. It's already shooting off in about one million directions. The creative potential to do just about any kind of music is there now, and all you've got to do is find the imagination to match it.(3)

More commercial acts have emerged since (The Grid, Enigma, Blue Pearl) that have attempted to bridge the gap between Ambient House and chart based dance markets, and their success suggests that the British music market is beginning to tune in to these modern ideas. *The Face* has also recently spoken of a New Age Mod (in stylistic terms admittedly) aware of technology, like the 'zippies', and publicising the trend with the denial that it is no 'mod revival'. The Grid have even collaborated with Timothy Leary in association with

162

the New Age publication *Evolution,* on a record decorated with all sorts of New Age, computer generated, surreal psychedelic imagery.

Progressive thinking is the key motive behind most of the recorded output of Ambient House. Ambient is defined in the dictionary as 'surroundings' which helps to explain the large amount of sampling from the environment and full use of recently developed technology. Sampling technology and new keyboard effects are being experimented with, echoing the goals that predominated during the psychedelic 60s (fusing new ideas with up to date technology) and the explorative motives of Pete 'Bassman' for example. The Shamen, however, extend this progressive thinking, reviving the 'anonymity' of artists and participants at events that made Acid House and raving initially so fresh. Their Synergy dance events have a drug connotation, as the word itself refers to the combined effect of drugs and organs, exceeding the sum of their individual effects. The events have no particular build up with the 'stars' (The Shamen) frequently coming on and off throughout the night DJ-ing, accompanying other DJs. Laser lights, strobes, oil slides and slide projections, and day-glo backdrops make the surrounding familiar to 60s style psychedelic events but, as guitarist Colin Angus points out, it is theoretically the anonymous rave atmosphere that forms the intention lying behind it:

> We're in the process of redefining the idea of a rock concert, with the intention of making it more like a club situation....It's a lot more than just not having gaps between the songs! We're emphasising the importance of making it like a club event, with a long show and continuous good quality sounds, light, visuals and performers...(4)

This dehumanising of traditional music 'icons', the performance, the songs and instrumentation, are all signs of a progressive acceptance of the powers of computerised technology that has increasingly been adapted into our societies, and now culture, since the late 50s (maybe even earlier, during the 19th century Industrial Revolution). The Shamen's use of digitalised, computer typography in silver and black on all their record sleeves and publicity emphasises their close relationship and dependence on digitalised technology. It would ultimately affect our record industries, with records being produced, recorded and pressed at a much faster rate. Which The Shamen believe will change marketing strategies, with 12" singles being released once a month (instead of every quarter) and two or three albums per year (rather than the usual 12-18 month gap). Note that this revolution is hypothetical only. These developments are isolated in an otherwise slowly adapting Western world. Others have expressed reservations about the longevity of New Age philosophies. Bobby Gillespie of Primal Scream (the band that·'tuned in' in late 1989) says:

> People in clubs aren't worrying about the ozone layer, they're just out for a good time....It's got nothing to do with flotation tanks and touching crystals to feel positive - that's just a few New Age entrepreneurs who are just trying to hijack the scene.(5)

Alison Shaw (singer of the experimental guitar band The Cranes) agrees with Gillespie's cynicism, "There's nothing wrong with a bit of escapism. But not everything's rosy, you can't just dance your life away." The link to the rave scene, a club scene where people escape from reality through dance and drugs, obviously undermines its present credibility to outsiders, but it persists by facing up to and using the latest technology in its production and execution.

The Shamen appear on stage (at the Synergy events) with televisions showing videos of fractal images, computer initiated spiral motifs first devised by mathematician Mandelbrot. These 'cyberdelic' spirals (cyber referring to the computer technology that creates them) resemble psychedelic art of the 60s and have increasingly begun to fascinate artists, designers and musicians. They appear in the videos and on the record covers of the Soup Dragons songs. The Grid used them on the cover of their collaboration with Timothy Leary and T-shirts depicting these designs have also been sold successfully by London firms such as Spacetime Ltd., who otherwise specialise in colourful knitwear. Their appeal lies in the beauty and intricacy of their colour harmonies and spiralling shapes, an aesthetic that also appealed to 60s hippies who had turned on the LSD experience. Marcus Pennell of *Evolution* magazine compares their importance to that of fine arts as "...these new organic paisleys will constitute the look of the 90s with as big an impact as Impressionism in its time."(7) Links to hippie philosophies also exist through these spirals' infinite character, having obvious connotations to the infinite nature of time, space and the universe. Patterns are generated by Mandelbrot's recurring mathematical equations, which action is infinite and therefore can symbolise the infinite nature and properties of the universe, space and time. The colour harmonies and shapes are formed by chance through a series of computations, the result of each having an impact on the next. There is no final result, as the computing equations are infinitely recurring and the shapes are constantly altering and growing out of one another, each formation having some consequence on the continually mutating whole. So these fractals do not just resemble the aesthetics and motifs found in psychedelic 60s poster art, but also reflect the philosophies surrounding psychedelic culture of the 60s and 90s. Like LSD, these spiralling patterns encourage us to reconsider our perception of mathematical dimensions, aesthetics and our relationship within the laws of the universe - without the unhealthy side effects of the synthetic substance.

There are also other machines that have recently emerged challenging our tepid acceptance of computer technology and even simulating a 'cosmic' state of mind, movement and action. Flotation Tanks, Virtual Reality and Dream Machines are all ways of transcending beyond conscious states of thinking and plugging directly into subconscious territory. Virtual Reality involves a computer presenting the individual with a computer generated landscape, seen through an 'Eyephone', and touch can be simulated through a 'Dataglove'. One could obviously draw a loose comparison between LSD's transcendental qualities and Virtual Reality, as Dorian Silver noted in an article on Cyberspace; "Americans are studying the psychological effects of placing humans in another world; just as LSD was tested on soldiers by the CIA in the sixties..."(8) But there are more practical possibilities for Virtual Reality than it simulating 'trips'. Architects can walk inside pre-built houses, the Japanese and others are planning to hold business meetings between business men thousands of miles apart, NASA's 'View' uses aspects of Virtual Reality to explore alien environments and doctors could possibly perform surgery without drawing blood.

Dream Machines, meanwhile, are more directly concerned with psychological health and rejuvenation. Together with Flotation Tanks they could be described as forms of computer aided meditation. They are light emitting devices that, at particular frequencies, stimulate brain waves which generally results in lightening the consciousness and aids relaxation (similar to traditional forms of meditation). These methods of inducing similar states of relaxation and mental autonomy that psychedelic drugs provoke, combine hippie philosophies with the practical use and acceptance of computer technology. Will these intentions degenerate into mere entertainment, or are they just novelty gadgets for a bohemian 'zippie' minority. A Swedish periodical, *Slitz*, recently reviewed the New Age Walkman, MC2, (a device that combines the Dream Machine, Eyephone and 'flipped out' synthesiser music to meditate to.) A character called Pepe Moreno in New York recently wrote and programmed the first fully computerised comic strip *Digital Justice*!! As these gadgets become more and more available it seems likely that misinterpretation and trivialisation will degenerate the real objectives - or maybe that kind of acceptance of computerised technology is as genuine as the 'zippies' acceptance of computers not just into their professions but also into their culture?

We discussed the effect of 'smart' drugs at the end of the "Fluke or Revolution?" section and ravers' response to healthier options of amassing dance energy, through natural energy replenishers, such as Guarana (some promoters even talked of sponsoring special 'G' nights rather than 'E' nights.) All of these New Age philosophies, the nature of Ambient House production, and computer simulated recreations of 'trip' experiences all show continual fascination with the effects of drugs, their positive aspects and general exploration. On the other hand, it also displays an awareness of not just the bad effects of drugs (with physical and ecological health now being preached, rather than drug induced highs) but also exploiting and maximising the benefits of the digital technology available, giving rise to new forms of artistic and musical expression. Most of the material discussed in this section admittedly has had less relation to design but the movement is still in its infancy. However, it is closely related to the spread of the dance 'craze' and, judging by the popularity of psychedelia recently on a commercial level, it promises to continue to develop. The fact that previously regressively styled Indie bands, Inspiral Carpets and Spacemen 3, have in March 1991 released House records (*Caravan* and *Big City* respectively) and the success of loosely Ambient sounding acts in the charts (Blue Pearl's *Naked in the Rain*, Enigma and Adamski's *Killer* - all Number 1's for a considerable period) could either be signs of the majority genuinely beginning to 'tune in', or else further 'bandwagon' attempts.

166

Whatever the motives, the essence of 60s psychedelia of exploring new technology and an open minded eclectic approach - wrapped loosely within some form of drug connotation - has returned to popular proportions.

Sources

1. Marcus Pennell (of *Evolution* magazine) quoted in 'New Science Meets New Age', *International Textiles*, No.716, September 1990, p.136.

2. Roger Morton, 'Cloud Cuckoo Man', *New Musical Express*, January 5, 1991, p.33.

3. Paul Lester, 'Shamen: Empire of the Senses', *Melody Maker*, September 15, 1990, p.46.

4. Ibid.

5. Retrospective 'That Was The Year That Was', *Melody Maker*, December 22/29, 1990, pp.70-71.

6. Ibid.

7. 'New Science Meets New Age', op cit, pp.136-138.

8. Dorian Silver and Alix Sharkey, 'Reality is Getting More Unreal Daily: Cyberspace', *The Face*, December 1990, pp.94-98.

Conclusion: Think about the phuture....

There have been a number of points that have emerged from this study which illustrates the state of current youth culture in Britain. The popular notion of eclecticism operating to market consumer products through novelty value and 'style' has been acknowledged but rejected by those who consider that process to be superficial and thus rendering each novel 'look' trivial and ultimately irrelevant to those who follow. Pete 'Bassman' and Alex 'Orb' Paterson spoke of an eclecticism that does not imitate but actually frees the imagination and inspires further creativity. One should add that exposure to drugs (in 'Bassman''s case) and new synthesiser technology (with 'The Orb') has enabled these objectives to come to some fruition - the same way LSD and new technology in the 60s liberated individual creativity and catalysed new forms of expression.

The vacuous 'fads' however, have succeeded in fragmenting youth culture by promoting the idea that whatever was 'hip' one month would only be supported by those 'hip' enough to be aware of those rapid changes, therefore giving them social credibility for their financial ability to support an elitist lifestyle. Punk was partly responsible too, for creating a Britain that respected the fact that anybody could make and issue music. It resulted in the spread of thousands of 'Indie'-pendent record labels all catering for small pockets of musical interest. But why should so many in a relatively well educated and sophisticated EC country follow these manufactured 'fads'? Judith Williamson's ideas about 80s consumerist tendencies in Britain cite a possible reason:

> It is the context of a society in which the majority of people have no control whatsoever over their productive lives : no security, little choice in work if they have work at all, and no means of public expression.(1)

Judith Williamson goes on to discuss the escapist tendencies which are an integral attraction within the consumerist process. These 'fads' were ways of escaping the dull, daily reality of living and working - particularly amongst the younger generation who were impressionable, fashion conscious, relatively inexperienced (giving them a better reason to imagine), and owned less (therefore firing a need to buy and assimilate both new and old material, but affording only the cheaper, disposable forms). These revivals prompted further reminiscence amongst the older generation as they saw their children relive *their* childhood in front of them. As the bulk of parents grew up in the 60s it was natural that that decade would be highlighted (although there were, of course, 50s, 70s revivals and 30s jazz revivals too).

The 60s and 80s were thus periods of indulgent escapism from harsh realities - drug induced escapism for explorative 'kicks'. Gadgets encouraged only further escapism and isolation, illustrated perfectly by the Walkman, an object allowing the user to escape from a "shared experience or environment."(2) Another reason why the 60s and 80s have been so closely aligned is due to the huge volume of studies undertaken and published on both those particular decades. Neither the 70s or the 50s have yet received so much attention as the former two. As commentators have analysed the 60s and 80s, and perhaps know comparatively more about them than any other periods, this may explain why there were so many parallels drawn between them. That would also explain the emergence of 'zippies' in the 90s who possess so much more *balance* in their attitudes towards drugs and new technology.

That 'balance' of heaven and hell or rationale, has not been clearly evident in any previous youth cultures. Most, if not all, degenerated into excessive versions of the initial purist objective; excess in popularity (the initial 'hip' specialised attraction becomes diluted by convention); excess in expression (repeating forms and patterns becoming 'samey'); excess in participation (with increased production comes more misinterpretation); and excess in marketing (by introducing it to an outside market the lifespan is considerably shortened due to those alien consumers' need for novelty and variety.) Is the current test for danceability doomed to burn itself out, through repetition, and be neatly replaced by an opposite? Are media discussions about New Age mods, punk revivals and 'zippies' signs of a reaction against the dance 'craze'? It would seem logical for a punk movement to recur as a natural reaction against the mellowed passivity, pacifism and drugs popularised by the dance 'craze' since 1986. In that case will that punk-esque trend react against the dehumanising process that has simultaneously occurred along with Acid House culture? The answer has traditionally come from America's ghetto culture, but Acid House represented a kind of liberation of Britain away from its over reliance on America. The

'90s may well derive from British ghettos in the shape of UK techno, where the bulk of experimental music flows from today, exceptions in America and Belgium acknowledged.

Sources

1.   Judith Williamson, *Consuming Passions, p.230.*

2.   Ibid, p.210.

Bibliography

Barnes, Richard, (ed.) *Mods,* Eel Pie Publications, 1979.

Booker, Christopher, *The Neo Philiacs: A Study of the Revolution in English Life in the 1950s and 1960s,* 1969.

Brody, Neville, *Sex, Drugs and Rock'n'Roll: A Pictorial History,* Bobcat Books, 1985.

Brown, Ashley, and Heatley, Michael, *Turning On: Rock in the Late Sixties,* Orbis, 1985.

Crosby, David, and Gottlieb, Carl, *Long Time Gone: Autobiography of David Crosby,* William Heinnemann, 1988.

Dalton, David, *The Rolling Stones: The First Twenty Years,* Alfred A. Knopf, 1981.

Gleason, Ralph, *Jefferson Airplane and The San Fransciscan Sound,* Ballantine, 1969.

Grushkin, Paul D., *Art of Rock: Posters from Presley to Punk,* Auberville, 1987.

Hebdige, Dick, *Subculture: The Meaning of Style,* 1979.

Herman, Gary, *Rock'n'Roll Babylon,* Plexus, 1982.

Huxley, Alduous, *Doors of Perception,* Penguin, 1988.

Joynson, Vernon, *The Acid Trip: A Complete Guide to Psychedelic Music,* Babylon Books, 1984.

Joynson, Vernon, *The Flashback: An Update of 'The Acid Trip',* Babylon Books, 1989.

MacGregor, Craig, *Pop Goes the Culture,* Pluto, 1984.

Marsh, David, *Before I Get Old: The Story of The Who,* Plexus, 1983.

Melly, George, *Revolt into Style*, 1970.

Murray, Charles Shaar, *Crosstown Traffic: Jimi Hendrix and Post-War Pop*, Faber and Faber, 1989.

Norman, Philip, *The Stones*, Elm Tree Books, 1984.

Redhead, Steve, *The End of Century Party*, Manchester University Press, 1990.

Reen, G. and Larue, M.,*Underground Graphics*, 1970.

Rolling Stone Magazine, 'What a Long Trip it's Been', *Rolling Stone*, 1987.

Scaduto, Anthony, *Mick Jagger*, W. H. Allen, 1974.

Sculatti, Gene, *San Franciscan Nights: The Psychedelic Music Trip*, St. Martin's Press, 1985.

Stevens, Jay, *Storming Heaven: LSD and the American Dream*, Paladin 1987.

Sugerman, Danny and Hopkins, Jerry, *No One Gets Out of Here Alive*, Plexus, 1980.

Taylor, Derek, *It Was Twenty Years Ago Today*, Bantam Press, 1987.

Thorgerson, S., *Classic Album Covers of the Sixties*, Paper Tiger, 1989.

Wells, Brian, *Psychedelic Drugs: Psychological, Medical and Social Issues*, Penguin, 1973.

Whitworth Art Gallery, *1966 and All That*, Manchester University Press, 1986.

Williamson, Judith, *Consuming Passions*, 1984.

Wolfe, Tom, *Electric Kool-Aid Acid Test*, Bantam Press, 1968.

Articles

Various periodicals were consulted during research, including *Melody Maker, The Face, New Musical Express, Sounds, Blitz, 20/20, i-D, Sunday Times Magazine, Boys Own* and *Slitz*. All articles used have been credited at the end of each section.

Additional sources

Additional material came from correspondence with various members of the current music and design industries. Contributors include:

Bassman, Pete - who is currently involved as bassist, songwriter and designer, with a well established Independent label band, The Darkside, on Situation Two Records.

Drew, Chris - commented on his design work for another Independent label group, Five Thirty, on WEA Records. Tragically, Chris Drew died during 1992, so my sympathies go to friends, relatives and the group Five Thirty. I am forever grateful for his cooperation and honest views expressed during the writing of this piece.

Mentzell, Nigel - who was a member of the original London underground psychedelic movement and is today a poster designer, selling original and reprinted 60s posters.

Redhead, Steve - author of the recent *The End of the Century Party*, has, with his colleagues, set up an archive of material in Popular Culture (offering a vast collection of rave flyers, posters and tickets, club promotions, football fanzines, as well as a selection of original 60s memorabilia for research purposes).

Smith, Paul - who attended most of the illegal raves of 1989 around Berkshire. Special thanks for his donation of several flyers illustrated in this publication.

Webbon, Steve - a member of the Independent label Beggar's

Banquet, who contributed his views on recent developments in British youth culture.

6 Drugs and popular music: The democratisation of bohemia

Patrick Mignon

"Let us ask in passing", notes Octavio Paz, "what would Baudelaire think of the socialisation of the Dandy in Carnaby Street? Our modernity is the inverse of his: we have made eccentricity a value of popular consumption."(1)

Paz is describing the transformation during the 20th century in the sheer extent of those protestations against the process of cultural equalisation and that theatricalisation of the tensions generated in the relationship between an individual and his/her social destiny, which is generally called the bohemian life.(2) In the 19th century, it was literature, theatre and painting that were the locations in which these acts of distancing were manifested, along with those tensions provoked by a critique of social conventions. Thus, it is in literature that the changing figure of drugs as means of action upon the self is expressed. This transformation of scale is also a change of vehicle, because the dress fantasies of Carnaby Street are rooted in the English pop group explosion of the early 60s.

In a society where cultural industries are developing and there is a widening of education, manifestations of bohemia increase, and music becomes the site par excellence in which these new representations acquire form. Thus, the increase in drug consumption in the second half of the 20th century is part and parcel of its omnipresence in rock and pop music, and of the adoption of the rock star as model for a new artistic lifestyle.

Two psychoactive products?

Popular music and drugs are two products which, by their very success, indicate the spread of behaviour previously reserved for the elites: the right to explore one's interior or social space. They are tied to the growth of the industries of dream and relaxation.

But the meeting of drugs and music is not a meeting of two psychoactive products each producing their own effects on body and soul. This idea of a power of music over the soul has a long history in the West. Music, like drugs, has several names: ragtime, jazz, rock n'roll, rock, etc. This diversity relates to the different ways they are defined, for groups or individuals, in order to face up to historical conjecture. This is why music must be analysed as a social world; that is, as an ensemble of practices, of values, of significations, of systems of valorisation and production. It is in such a social world that drugs intervene as one of the elements of its definition. In effect, drugs may occupy a place which is functional - as an aid to work or a means of bearing its load - and, at a symbolic level, be an expression of a relationship to the world, allowing us to examine certain contradictions in its musical project. Music encounters drugs when the experience of drugs accompanies the accession to the musical and cultural avant-guard, when the definition of the musician as artist renders necessary the manipulation of the ensemble of signs of his election; drugs encounter music when they are the necessary component of a way of life of certain sub-groups, when they form part of the definition of what the good life is.

This musical world is attractive to the extent that its workings and its myths constitute a reference for those seeking spaces which respond to the uncertainties of their social situation. You build with what you can find; you discover music as a body of, more or less, explicit discourses and sounds, practises and objects, of places and networks to which one can turn when questions arise concerning your social identity. You turn to the hidden continent of popular music, the music and the traditions which provide you with a permanent source of renewal.

This world is constituted in the quest for new aesthetic emotions; that which is known, and that which is imagined, of a music, that with which you engage when you discover the properties of a new sonority. When this quest is at the centre of the preoccupations and practices of a musical milieu, music naturally encounters drugs. In its systematic search for innovation, popular music tries to discover new worlds; in its means of distribution it brings to light or dramatises those milieus or subcultures who live extra-ordinary lives, outside social conventions.

Two accesses are possible to drugs through music: via the musical message in which the effects are described, and via life histories of the artist, dramatising the models of behaviour or signs of singularity belonging to marginality or celebrity. The social world of music, under its precise form of jazz or rock - when it divides the world into that which is authentic and that which is not, or when it emphasises ideals of self-accomplishment - presents, in a most spectacular way, all the possibilities of escaping your social destiny, by the creation of the self and of an *oeuvre.* That which the maker of music (who can be a musician, but also producer or manager) realises, so too does the consumer in the care which s/he takes in choosing that which s/he consumes.

The history of the relations between drugs and popular music is the history of a variation on the various themes of bohemia - that could be understood in the general sense of a theatricalisation, a distanciation of the social world and its conventions; taking the form of dandyism, the elitism of poverty or the fascination with failure.(3) It is also the history of a democratisation of bohemia, of the massive extension of the theatricalisation of incertitude.

This history unfolds in two phases.(4) Firstly, in the restricted, and always elitist, context of the identification with a particular community, that of black Americans and their music. This is - in its 'folk' form - jazz lived as expression of a natural nobility, or - in its 'artistic' form - jazz as the quest for beauty. Then later, there is the more massive context of the development of rock music. Here, if the frontiers of bohemia and the conventional world tend to dissolve, the different responses to the uncertainties of social destiny illustrate the diversity of uses and significations found in the same product.

The autonomisation of music

Drugs and jazz: Vocations of pleasure (1880-1914)

The workings of popular music, notably the competition amongst the producers of this music and their quest for innovation, are at the root of the discovery of new musical and social worlds. In this context, music discovered drugs because they are commonly used by musicians or because they are tied to the way of life of exotic and fascinating populations, in this instance the blacks, who represent lost nature or excess.

Urbanisation and the waves of internal and external immigration threw into the cities of America individuals in quest of the pleasures of sociability and constant innovation. The industries of health care, medicine and pharmacy, and the industries of pleasure, of which music formed part, were two expressions of this movement of modernisation: newspapers profited largely from advertisements for medicines, and the music industry, which was known at the time as Tin Pan Alley, produced its first millionaires.

The development of the pharmaceutical and music industries meant inevitably the development of their margins. To the rationalisation of the 'quest for excitement',(5) the production of dreams and the development of new spaces of sociability, of relaxation and comfort, was opposed the search for new frontiers. Medicine and Tin Pan Ally produced their discontented, those who couldn't recognise themselves in the romance and moralism of the hit songs, or those who wanted to get well quicker or use the medicines in different ways. They also had their marginals in search of profits and new inspirations. The press was financed by recognised medicine; the 'medicine shows' and the miracle doctors had their own distinct means of promotion, reliant on the seductions of music.

The Medicine Show was a travelling spectacle, allowing, as it crossed the countryside, those populations who knew nothing of the charms of urbanity to partake of the new miracle cures. It attracted onlookers by offering them music as played in New York, or that which they were used to hearing, country music or blues. The relationship which was established at that moment between drugs and music was a functional one. For itinerant spectacles were usually a question of drugs: cocaine and morphine formed the base of many of these miracle cures. Thanks to the medicine shows a musical milieu emerged which guaranteed to amateur musicians the means to professionalisation or, for the quasi-professional, the means to escape the rigours of the urban life. So were created those images of the life of the musician wrapped in the experience of powerful sensations: the dangers of itinerancy and racism, the liberty of the nomad, drugs and alcohol. The blues musician sang of herbs and roots which gave strength and health, and everywhere he carried with him his 'mojo bag', full of the golden leaves of Mexico. The bluesmen or the jazzmen thus represented the music of the devil and of liberty - first of all a figure within the black community, soon becoming one for young whites. These spectacles thus constituted one of the bases of the emergent mythology of the popular musician, that of life on the margins, and the repertory of the singers was largely concerned with descriptions of aspects of this life.

The more sedentary musicians who lived in the big cities could not always be distinguished from other professionals of pleasure: the ragtime or jazz musician was at the same time professional player, charlatan, procurer and dealer. New Orleans, the city of crossroads, which mixed together blacks, whites, Mexicans and Antillans, symbolised this situation. There was a big welcome for those Mexican or Porto Rican traders who, thanks to the virtues of 'muta', 'greefa', and 'reefer', gave the black population a chance to reactivate memories of African society and the whites a chance to taste of forbidden pleasures. Vice was mobile, embarking on the paddle boat steamers or on the trains which went up the Mississippi. They got off in Memphis, Saint Louis, in Chicago and New York, with their instruments and their mojo bags.

The whole history of Jazz began tied to the seductions of a life outside the law. During prohibition the night clubs, run by the mafia, harboured the big names of the period in the name of a community of outsiders of American society, and in that of the seduction of the margins. Here illegal alcohol and drugs circulated.

New born, then triumphant, jazz was thus two things: the social danger represented by Sambo, the simple black from the medicine show, becoming Satan and personifying all the menaces of sexual permissiveness and violence, especially when under the influence of drugs. The image of the black is tied to that of drugs (like the Chinese had been previously) in so far as marijuana or cocaine were rather more commonly used than amongst other sections of the population - doubtless because cocaine formed part of the plantation pharmacy, used increase the energy of weakening slaves. The Blackman was Bogeyman. But American blacks were also symbols of a lost nature, the holders of an unknown power, and also, in the form of the itinerant blues musician, a romantic figure, symbol of a free life.

For a young white breaking free,(6) whether he preferred the street or the billiard hall to school and the straight and narrow, the black ghetto offered the possibility of listening to real hot music. King Oliver or Louis Armstrong provided this model of the beautiful life. To defy the American way of life was to plunge into black music and jazz; to become a musician was to discover the secret language of drugs and music; grass gives energy, the desire to play, to listen to what the others play and play with them, to eat well and never sleep. Grass and music allow one to be cool, to have a good time and get through all eventualities. Jazz sings, for the initiated, of 'joints' - Louis Armstrong's *Muggles* goes through all the names for marijuana (Mary Rosa, Mary Warner), the dealer (*Reefer Man* by Cab Calloway), pleasures shared (*Tea for Two*, in jazz and musical comedy), etc. Jazz is both rupture and an entrance into the bohemian life, into a community which grass, and the slang to which it gives birth, consolidates and protects against the outside.

Jazz and drugs formed part of that simultaneous discovery "of a music which fills a void", according to the words of Jean Cocteau who found there his own hallucinatory practice. What void? Michel Leiris has described it:

> In that period of great permissiveness which followed the hostilities, jazz was a rallying point, an orgiastic standard in the colours of the moment. It operated magically and its mode of influence can be compared to a possession. It was the element which could best give sense to those celebrations, a religious meaning in which communion was through dance, eroticism - latent or manifest - and drink, the most effective means of closing the gulf that separates individuals from each other wherever they meet. Pounded by the violent blasts of hot air from the tropics, jazz had within it enough of the stenches of a dead civilisation, of a humanity submitting blindly to the machine, to express as completely as it was possible to do, the states of mind of at least some of us: a more or less conscious demoralisation coming from the war, naive astonishment before the mod cons and dernier cries of progress, the current taste for decoration, the inanity of which we had a confused foreboding, an abandonment to the animal joy of submission to

the influence of modern rhythm, an aspiration underlying a new life where a large place would be given to that savage innocence for which we ravenously desired, though this was still yet unformed. The first appearance of blacks, myth of coloured edens which would lead me to Africa and, beyond Africa, towards ethnography.(7)

Bohemia: Jazz and the beats

With the end of prohibition a rupture occurred in the world of jazz musicians. The closure of the big clubs spelt the end of the big orchestras and an easy living: positions became hard to find and record and radio competed with public spectacles. The new black musicians also defined themselves differently. They were no longer 'entertainers' but artists who effected a double rupture; opposed to the white world and to the conventional world such as that valorised by Mezz Mezzrow.

In *The fever for life*, Mezzrow uncovered other drugs; opium, heroin, but also alcohol. He had tried alcohol and opium: opium stops you doing anything, and during the five years as an opium taker he couldn't be bothered to pick up a single instrument. Alcohol opened up another world and another music - aggressive, mistrustful, artificial, a long way from his own jazz. For him the new jazz - swing or be-bop - was music coming from an internal chaos, wild and crazy. He also alludes to the rise of other drugs amongst the jazzmen, and one thinks of Charlie Parker. But he also thinks of Bix Beiderbeck, who preferred alcohol to grass and didn't see jazz as an entrance to a new, more balanced world, but as a painful ordeal in order to tear himself out of white America; election is in failure.

Two destinies, two opposed conceptions of jazz music; jazz as folk music, whose tastes and practices were now aimed at integration within a new people and at the sharing of its pleasures; and jazz as art, that is, as the risk of being misunderstood. Mezzrow's jazz was, for the new musicians, the creators of be-bop, a form of 'uncle-tomism', a reduction of blacks to the level of Sambo. Be-bop would be a claim for artistic necessity, in a situation of uncertainty as regards employment and the social identity of the musician.

The new drug, which spread throughout the 40s and 50s, was heroin. This drug appeared as a way of putting some order into the social and aesthetic uncertainties which characterised the new jazz musicians. The effects emphasised most were those that produced a 'cool' attitude and a detachment enabling them to cope with the contradictions of their situation: being amongst the avant-guard, marking off the boundary between the ordinary world and the extraordinary world of creation, intensifying, by the will to control over the self and the drug, the will to master ones artistic project, but also intensifying, in the competition for heroin, the competitiveness which set musicians against one another. Music, like drugs, demands that one goes further; to stay out there, and become a myth, or to return and become a hero, he who has survived through all ordeals.

The consumption of drugs is equally a means of consolidating a milieu and establishing a routine necessary to support the randomness of getting work and musical creation. To enter the world of jazz is to enter music through the initiation of the jam session, where the ability of the candidate is judged by his skill in playing with the others. To enter the world of jazz is also to enter the world of drugs. The musicians always had with them their little bags with all the necessary instruments of consumption; but the musician's milieu was also surrounded by those who supplied the drugs. The aspiring candidate often met the dealer before he met the musician, and experiencing cocaine and heroin gave him some hope that he could accede to that double secret of improvisation and the language of the community of musicians. The community of heroin takers reinforced the community of musicians; the rituals of music and the rituals of drugs were equally elements of the sociability and the definition of the jazz world. It defined itself in relation to the limits of the musical system (playing with rhythm and the tonal system), to the limits of life and death, and to the limits of legality. One's election as artists is demonstrated equally well by both commercial failure and imprisonment.

But the integration of heroin into the jazzmen's way of life can also be seen in terms of its practical advantages; it doesn't stop one from playing and it protects against the minor illnesses which hamper the life of the musician, such as colds and flu - or at least eliminate the symptoms. This function is another version of the relationship between music and drugs; drugs exist also as drugs for working, and in this sense they are not drugs but remedies against minor physical ailments, and anxiety.(8)

In the black experience art and heroin are ways of escaping white society. But the road which leads young whites towards jazz, and towards heroin, is always one of the desire to join a black society seen as a negation of the principles of white society. It is thus that drugs and music - jazz and folk both - found their literary expression with the 'beat generation'. The beat writers Burroughs and Ginsberg set down the conditions of the quest for another life and an exit from bureaucratic society: journeys in exterior or interior spaces, the ideal of self-mastery or loss of that self, and the fascination with failure.

The writing of Kerouac and Burroughs, in their desire to shock, was

> an uninterrupted cascade, from the depths of the soul, of ideas and words blown along by images; no full stops separate the phrases - ridiculous punctuations - but vigorous blanks separate the rhetorical breathing; not selectivity of expression, but the acceptance of free associations produced by the mind in a sea without limits, swimming in a sea of English without any other discipline than that of the rhetorical breathing and the clarifications like a fist banging the table

etc., all of it interspersed with "like a saxophonist".(9)

In its popular form, with the emergence of 'beatniks', going to clubs to hear jazz and folk, and to consume anything that could derange the senses (most usually marijuana, alcohol and amphetamines) becomes part of an explicit project of a practical contestation of the values of capitalist, technocratic society.

Drugs in mass culture

The 60s were years of a massive eruption of drugs. However, if one mostly has the image of grass, of hippies and LSD, of counter-cultural values, this also involved other products inscribed within a different process.

The loser: Rock 'n' roll and amphetamines

The eruption of rock n'roll in the 50s was by no means part of the wake produced by jazz or the beat generation. Drugs were a completely invisible object within rock n'roll. Nevertheless, besides the exhausting tours which encouraged taking something to keep on going, rock n'roll involved models of behaviour which made alcohol and drugs the necessary ingredients of a certain way of life. To the literary bohemian was opposed the bohemia of country music, and then of rock n' roll. This figure did not form part of the explicit media image but it fed into the representation of that rock n'roll lifestyle.

The idea of transgression, which nourished the representations of the beat generation, was alien to the culture of rock n'roll in the 50s. Even if it defined itself through references and codes hermetically sealed from the adult world, the rock n'roll of the time reproduced, nevertheless, the expansive dynamic of American society. The constitutive givens of that society (car, money, women) were not rejected but invested with a will to live lacking in the adult world. There was no thematisation of drugs because rock n'roll set itself itself to discovering American society and participating in the American dream. But we also know that what we call rock n'roll reflects quite different places and contexts: its most popular form is white, but its original forms are more precise - black and southern. If the myth of rock n' roll had a meaning, if it could mature and if one could mature within rock n'roll, then, this was not one of youth but of life on the road and the secret of live fast, work hard, die young. The consumption of alcohol and amphetamines acquire their meaning in this perspective, where work is an essential part of drunkenness or getting high.

The first rock n'roll was a music of hoodlums. One thinks of Selby and his first novel *Last Exit to Brooklyn*: delinquents around the jukebox, the sailor hunt and the various pills they constantly swallow. But, above all, the territory of rock n'roll, in its rockabilly form, is the South. That which became rock n'roll developed in this context because a new popular music can only be born in a region which maintains strong musical traditions. This is the case with the southern states which were identified with country music and contained a large proportion of the black population.

In the South appear contradictory aspects, where drugs are one of the elements of an ambivalence towards social conventions. The Second World War had given those who had been demobilised the choice of going to University, thanks to the 'G.I. Bill'. Many ex-soldiers, especially in the South, became 'truckers' in order to realise the dream of a free life spent crossing the great open spaces. These truckers were at the same time symbols of individualist values and the heirs to the rebel tradition of the South, where the maintenance of the fundamental values of virility and honour was so much defiance of Yankee ideology. They constituted the hard core of country music fans and gave a living to the musicians who travelled the country from bar to bar: in these noisy spaces was invented, in part, a music capable of grabbing the listeners attention by the the systematic use of amplification. The road, alcohol, stimulants, all were part of the tradition of country music and its stars: for the South was equally the country of clandestine alcohol - a traditional defiance of authority by small communities jealous of their independence - and of the trafficking of amphetamines necessary to keep rolling along with your truck. As in the time of the Medicine Show, drugs represented a tie between spectators and musicians: they shared the same codes - notably the valuation of work, symbol of virility and honour - and the musician participated in the same culture of stimulants, part of the culture of hard work. Often, moreover, they would receive amphetamines as tips. Nevertheless, in this fever of work to be done - driving or playing music - there was always the risk of exhaustion, or going too far: country musicians - and certain rockabilly musicians later on - would die in the attempt (alcohol, stimulants and exhaustion from touring, like Hank Williams) or cause a scandal by their violence (Jerry Lee Lewis) - thereby tracing another figure, that of an excess of commitment, as much to their public as to a task to be accomplished.

Rock and the expansion of minds

The pursuit of the 'beat' quest for the beyond continued. A new invention was added to the well known products: LSD. First used in 1943 in research into schizophrenia and experimented with in American universities, it was the site of an encounter between scientists (Timothy Leary) and the bohemian world of literature (Ginsberg) and music (John Coltraine). Research into the brain was tied to an exploration of the mind and to an analysis of the drug's social effects.

Before descending onto the street and becoming the psychedelic drug par excellence, LSD was the object of a passionate debate amongst the first experimenters.(10) In view of its gigantic powers, should it stay in the hands of a scientific and intellectual elite, or

185

should one encourage its consumption, initiating the maximum numbers in order to feel its social and cultural effects as quickly as possible? Its adepts chose the route of democratisation: the bus driven by Ken Kesey carrying the Merry Pranksters for two years (1964-65) along the highways of America, created a sensation wherever it visited. The lights and the sounds of the rock group that went with them, The Warlocks - future Grateful Dead's - accompanied collective acid taking. Settled in San Francisco they animated the various 'love ins' and 'be ins' that mobilised, in parks and campus, the new figure of bohemia: the hippy.

It is in these circumstances that psychedelic music was born, clearly inscribing drugs and music in a movement of reciprocity and mutual enrichment. Music accompanied the ceremonies of LSD initiation, or tried to share with participant the experiences of the musician. In this relation of equivalence rock is carried by a mimetic ambition to recreate the atmosphere of hallucination or use distortions likely to produce effects similar to those of LSD. Rock was not the only player in this competition to act upon minds: the improvisations of free jazz and sonorities of Indian music were part of a similar project.

Rock, from 1965 onwards, offered a series of drug songs: The Byrds (*Mr. Tambourine Man*) and Dylan (*Everybody Must Get Stoned*), but also the Beatles, after the Dylan-Beatles encounter, with *Strawberry Fields, Yellow Submarine, Lucy in the Sky....* Here, the musical arrangement and the esoteric lyrics - according to one astute observer at of this period - only allowed of two methods by which to decipher them: the recourse to drugs through which you could enter a universe created by their means - or a Ph.D. But offered to everyone - courtesy of a joint and a 33 rpm album - eternity in an hour:

To see the world in a grain of sand
and heaven in a wild flower
To hold eternity in the palm of your hand
and eternity in an hour
(William Blake)

The dynamics of drugs

The emergence of drugs as a useful tool in the alteration of consciousness signifies the entrance of the bohemian tradition into mass culture, with all the tensions that this brings with it.

You needed a Ph.D or to take drugs in order to understand both rock and the counter-culture because they were a secret - so they said ("And something is happening and you don't know what it is, do you, Mr. Jones" - Bob Dylan) The problem was that this secret did not oppose those who knew - the young, to those who didn't - the adults: it opposed those who knew, the leaders, the theoreticians, the propagandists, the artists that one had to wait for, to those who did the waiting. This secret that one had to penetrate gave rise to the establishment of a whole industry of rapid initiation.

Psychedelia was also huge concert halls with big projectors; that is to say, the popularisation of initiation. Communal control is strong when the adepts are close to each other and there still exists something resembling initiation. But the massive arrival of drop-outs in San Francisco returned the encounter with drugs to the street - to the competition between dealers and to the disassociation of the different experiences. Psychedelic music undoubtedly referred to drugs, but the experience of drugs was no longer a controlled experience. The workshops of Augustus Owsley, the manufacturer who guaranteed his products, were succeeded - especially after his arrest in 1967 - by a multitude of small scale artisans or manufacturers, and by a traffic in amphetamines, under their two forms of stimulant and tranquilliser.

Two events that occurred a few months apart are symbolic of this separation between two different relationships with drugs: Woodstock, where they could brag about having controlled the products which were circulating and of celebrating three days of peace, love and music; and Altamont, where the frightening atmosphere in which the concert took place and the murder of a spectator, were insuperable from the quasi-accidental convergence of counter-cultural students and teenagers from the working class areas, that is to say, two conceptions of time (a free time which opens out within a permanent leisure as against a constrained time) and the drug habits which go with them; that of LSD and that of amphetamines and alcohol.

The secret of the liberation of minds was for others a means of coping with the big concert crowds and the pressure of communal needs. It is in this sense that we can interpret the spreading use of tranquillisers at hard rock concerts; a physical preparation for a sound which became more and more effective with the progress of

187

amplification, and at the same time, a means of creating islands within the mega-concert crowds, thus producing that atmosphere of suppressed anger and the transformation of good vibrations into barbed wire.

This same tension is perceptible in the use of amphetamines in Andy Warhol's 'Factory'. Here it derives from the frantic competition on which the Warholian system functioned. The logic of celebrity and the Factory hierarchy demanded amphetamines in order to stay alert, to seize the occasions for being seen or participating in something. In New York, at the height of the epoch of counter-culture, the logic of competition explicitly dominated this scene and reflected, in opposition to the millenarian dreams of the hippies, the universe of the dereliction of a great city. The tour of the west in 1966 by the rock group launched by Warhol, The Velvet Underground, shocked the partisans of counter-culture, by its insistent, monotonous music and the perversions which it described. For more or less the whole of this period, through his representative figures, Warhol, but also Lou Reed, opposed to the easy-going hippies a chemically sustained impassivity and coolness.

Poses and styles: Mods and punks

Next to the counter-culture there existed subcultures. In the English context, they refer to those coherent ensembles of objects, values and practices originating in a class culture - borrowing some elements but aiming to distance this culture at the same time. The recent history of Great Britain has paraded a multiplicity of these formations, from the hooligans of the 19th century to the teddy-boys, mods, skinheads, punks, etc. all articulated in terms of clothes, music and drugs.

The notion of subculture is ambiguous. It contains one bias which leans towards a tribal interpretation of subculture, seen as a system closed within itself, and another which privileges the aspect of *bricolage* and refuses their systematic nature - arguing that it is academics, ideologists and cultural observers who produce these subcultures. However, even if we may doubt the systematic character of subcultures, they condense, at certain moments, the characteristics of particular groups.

There is little known about drugs use amongst teddy-boys or rockers. We know about alcohol, notably beer, which constituted one of the elements necessary for the affirmation of virility. As for drugs, one could hypothesise that they took amphetamines, whose consumption was relatively common in Great Britain, notably amongst certain marginal groups such as prostitutes or young delinquents. Through a stylisation which combined attention to clothes, to hairstyle, and maintaining the image of the western gambler, the teddy boys imposed in their dandyism an image of a refusal of the degradation of their condition. The rocker, in accentuating the rough side - and, when a biker, the defiance of death - played with the image of the Loser.

The figure of the mod is better known. The tradition of 'Modernists' derives from the end of the 50s when, in the Soho nightclubs, one listened to jazz, smoked marijuana and took speed after the fashion of the bohemian beatnik. Here, at least as important as the figure of the black American, was the Jamaican rude boy, the bad boy of the Kingston ghettos transplanted to London. The principle of the rude boy, always correctly dressed - suit, little hat, dark glasses - was to be able to stay cool, to know how to resist the pressure; that is to say, to impose oneself without violence, to say nothing to the police and to indulge in small scale dealing. Jamaican coolness is brought by grass, but without the mystical content given to it some years later by the Rastas.

The mod explosion in the middle of the 60s was inspired, in terms of its musical tastes and (in part) its clothes, by the coolness of the rude boys. Coming from the working class, the mods emphasised social mobility and a commitment to the consumer society, contrary to the teddy boys and rockers who claimed a proletarian destiny, even if it was to be achieved through style. In this engagement amphetamines played a fundamental role. After a week of work they allowed you to cope with the week-end, going wherever it took you, buying records, clothes, going to a nightclub or concert and dancing all night. The mod was a model of the well-informed consumer, choosing the rare discs and required clothes because he was in competition with the rockers and with other mods. The effects of speed were an integral part of the stakes involved in being a 'face', a character who imposes himself by his appearance alone and causes those who cannot stand up to him to flee in shame: keeping up the pose, nervousness, suppressed aggression...to crash out only on Sunday night.

To speak of a musical thematisation of amphetamine use would be wrong, apart from a hit song from a leading mod group, The Small Faces, glorifying the dealer. But The Who, above all, were in step with them, by a nervous music in which the impossibility of communication and the tension or difficulty of keeping up appearances is continually affirmed. The mods were also, in terms of bands and their appearance, a product of the art schools, of the balancing of popular success and the command of an artistic project.

Punks were, more explicitly than the mods, adepts of amphetamines. The target was the easy-going nature of the hippy, symbolised by hashish or drugs involving control such as LSD - which presupposes gurus. The virtue of speed was always that it allowed you to stay alert and to hold yourself taut, a way of hardening your look at the same time as grinding your teeth. As regards drugs at the time, they were integrated into an aesthetic of scandal and shock, represented as much by the primitive music as by the foregrounding of cuts and wounds characteristic of punk. A movement made as much by stylists and apprentice artists as by the unemployed, punk culture was also a subculture where to be a 'face' and to know how to keep up that face, was of the utmost importance.

Acid house and the dissolution of bohemia?

The logic of punk was auto-dissolution: the aesthetics of shock cannot survive repetition. No figure attempted to endure in order to give lessons to society and thus punk pointed to the dissolution of every bohemia. But the capacity to survive in the face of the world, to create yourself, your own clothes, your own music, to be independent, all these are lessons. In this sense the recent acid-house movement has realised this 'do-it-yourself' project: home-based electronic equipment and sampling allow the production of your own music using the most heterogeneous musical sources. Everyone has their turn, disc-jockeys can become stars. Moreover, the new drug Ecstasy, is clever enough to possess the hallucinatory qualities of LSD and the energetic qualities of amphetamines, whilst minimising the need for initiation and certain secondary effects, notably aggression. It has a universal vocation: it goes with proletarian cafe crawls in Spain or dancing in Manchester, as well as the activities of the new professionals; it calms the hooligans and it is not clear yet if there is any barrier of age. In this movement, the frontiers (age, race, class, danger) which allow the definition of a bohemian space give the impression of no longer existing.

Popular music has been for several decades the channel whereby those preoccupations which belong to avant-guard art are democratised. The joint effects of the spread of education and academia, of the growth of cultural industries, and the expansion of consumption have rendered less evident and less pertinent all that which separated the hedonist world of bohemia from the bourgeois world. The ideal of making oneself visible, of being yourself and doing it yourself, is no longer the privilege of a minority. In this sense, Acid House, and the interpretations which are given it, or that it gives itself, can symbolise the end of bohemia. But this new alliance of music and drugs is a utopia, that of permanent changing of identity - without the risk. it is a defiant challenge and a new frontier.

Sources

1. Courant Alternatif, Paris 1972, p.60.

2. See especially Cesar Grana, *Bohemians versus Bourgeois,* (1964), New York. Jerrold Siegel, *Bohemian Paris,* (1986), New York, Viking.

3. According to the terms used by Cesar Grana.

4. For a detailed history of the relations between pop music and drugs see: Harry Shapiro, *Waiting for the Man: The Story of Drugs and Popular Music,* (1986), London.

5. In English in the original.

6. See Mezz Mezzrow, *La Rage de Vivre,* Paris, Livre de Poche.

7. In *L'Age d'homme,* Paris, Livre de Poche, p.185.

8. For example, it has been remarked upon (*The Observer,* May 10, 1990), that musicians in classical orchestras were amongst the biggest consumers of psychoactive products, in large part in order to face up to the demands of excellence in their musical work.

9. Tod Gitlin, *The Sixties, Years of Hope, Days of Rage,* (1987), New York.

10. See Jay Stevens, *Storming Heaven: LSD and the American Dream,* (1987), New York.

Translated by Justin O'Connor, from an article which was originally published in French in *Esprit* in 1991.